CW00922798

BLACK BELT KARATE

BLACK BELT KARATE

The Intensive Course

Hirokazu Kanazawa

PRESIDENT OF Shotokan Karate-do International Federation

FOREWORD BY Masatoshi Nakayama

TRANSLATED BY Richard Berger

KODANSHA INTERNATIONAL
Tokyo • New York • London

Pronouncing Japanese

The Japanese terms appearing in this book have been written in accordance with the modified Hepburn romanization system. With only five vowel sounds, the pronunciation of Japanese is not overly difficult once the pronunciation of each vowel has been learned.

Each vowel is pronounced as follows:

a — *ah*, as the "a" in father
e — *eh*, as the "e" in get
i — *ee*, as the "ee" in feet
o — *oh*, as the "o" in go
u — *ooh*, as the "oo" in food

Vowels with a mark above them (as in the words *jōdan* and *chūdan*) indicate lengthened vowels. They are pronounced in the same fashion as their shorter counterparts but last a little longer when spoken.

For information concerning the Shotokan Karate-do International Federation, please refer to the below:

2–1–20 Minami-Kugahara
Ota-ku, Tokyo
146–0084 Japan
PHONE: 81–(0)3–3754–5481   FAX: 81–(0)3–3754–5483
E-MAIL: japan@skif.jp

Jacket photos and all step-by-step photos by Naoto Suzuki. Calligraphy by the author.

Techniques are demonstrated by the author, Shigeyuki Ichihara, Manabu Murakami, Nobuaki Kanazawa, Ryusho Suzuki, Shinji Tanaka, Fumitoshi Kanazawa, Daizo Kanazawa, and Yoko Kubokura.

Originally published in Japanese as *Karate: Rokushūkan de Tsuyokunaru* by Ikeda Shoten in 1978.

Distributed in the United States by Kodansha America, Inc., and in the United Kingdom and continental Europe by Kodansha Europe Ltd.

Published by Kodansha International Ltd., 17–14 Otowa 1-chome, Bunkyo-ku Tokyo 112–8652, and Kodansha America, Inc.

First edition, 2006
15 14 13 12 11 10 09 08 07 06   12 11 10 9 8 7 6 5 4 3 2 1

www.kodansha-intl.com

CONTENTS

CHAPTER 4
Arm-Leg Combinations, Kata and Basic Free-Sparring

CHAPTER 5
From Self-Defense to Nunchaku

Chapter 6
Building Future Training Menus

FOREWORD

TO THE ORIGINAL JAPANESE EDITION

Movements that are in keeping with the natural flow, that are free of wasted motion. A variety of techniques delivered in succession, each linking seamlessly with the next and transforming in new and unexpected ways—Mr. Kanazawa employs a diverse range of such combination techniques. While a member of the Takushoku University karate team, he applied himself with great diligence to extremely grueling physical and mental training in karate's three essential areas of *kihon* (basics), *kata* (from), and *kumite* (sparring), making "Kanazawa of Takushoku" a revered figure among members of opposing university karate teams.

In the spring of 1956, upon graduating from university, he turned down the job that had been awaiting him after my suggestion that he devote himself to karate, and became one of the first A-list instructor trainees at the then newly established Japan Karate Association.

I can only assume that his desire to pursue a career as a karate instructor, a path whose destination we were not certain of at the time, must have been great indeed. Needless to say, I am filled with joy that he actually took me up on the (quite unreasonable) proposal that I offered him. I can think of no one better suited to adorn the first page of karate-dō history, having achieved the glory of being a pioneer in the Japan Karate Association's trainee program, which played a key role in the advancement of karate-dō and the remarkable global popularity that the sport currently enjoys.

Mr. Kanazawa also played a supporting role in karate's landmark development as a competitive sport, making an impressive showing at the world of karate-dō's first-ever major Japan championship tournament by taking first place in the *kumite* division. And then, prior to leaving for Hawaii as an overseas instructor, he followed the performance the next year by winning not only in the *kumite* division, but also in the *kata* division, achieving one of karate's rare overall victories.

At the second tournament he faced fellow JKA trainee Takayuki Mikami in a heated bout that was so impressive it is still talked about today. The match was truly a thing of beauty, with Mr. Kanazawa displaying a variety of expert techniques comprising punches, strikes, and kicks. He launched dynamic attacks while freely shifting forward and backward, left and right, coordinating each technique with the movement of his body. Upon attacking, he would anticipate his opponent's response, immediately change tack, and move in for the kill using a different technique. From motion to stillness, stillness to motion—these transitions were truly remarkable.

Such impressive techniques and moves, however, cannot be mastered overnight. They can only be acquired through day after day of hard work and training in the basics.

Without a physical and mental commitment to discipline and training, there is no hope for improvement. Additionally, it is essential to remember that effective training can only be realized when the guidance and advice offered by qualified instructors are faithfully carried out, as such instruction has been derived from valuable experience acquired over a long period of time.

In this respect, in the writing of this book, Mr. Kanazawa has fully applied his valuable experience and taken great pains to organize an impressive guide that presents a sensible approach to acquiring the essential skills of karate.

By following each and every page of this book as if receiving instruction directly from Mr. Kanazawa, I believe that over time, with careful practice, gaining proficiency is all but guaranteed. For anyone setting out to master karate-dō, you hold in your hands a fine book indeed.

Masatoshi Nakayama

Former Chief Instructor, Japan Karate Association
(Mr. Nakayama passed away on April 15, 1987)

PREFACE

Power comes from the lower abdomen, techniques from the hips

To become strong; to develop beautiful, lithe muscles; to maintain health and longevity; to feel cheerful and refreshed—people start down the path of karate for a variety of reasons.

Karate is a martial art that can be practiced by anyone, regardless of age or sex, and can be begun at any time during a person's life.

No matter how different one's entry into the world of karate may be, with untiring perseverance, all of the original objectives behind the decision to start training can be achieved. Also, without even realizing it, the day will come when that person discovers that he is able to remain level-headed in the face of almost any occurrence. This is the allure of karate, and the road that leads to becoming a black belt. It is also the road that leads to mastery of the art.

Karate is a theoretical approach to physical training for the mind and body that adheres to the physical laws of the universe. By systematically training the arms and legs, it also becomes a means of self-defense that offers benefits in our everyday lives. While it goes without saying that karate is ideal as a means of gymnastic exercise, as a sport, and as a form of mental training, it also offers physiological benefits. By training the lower abdomen—our gravity center (called *tanden* or *seika-tanden* in Japanese; located in the lower belly below the navel)—and employing proper breathing techniques (thoracic respiration, abdominal respiration, lower-abdominal respiration), we are able to achieve mental concentration and cultivate *ki* (life energy), the very root of human life, thus facilitating the generation of energy essential for good health and living.

Since I was in my teens, I have devoted all of my time to karate. And even now, at the age of 74, I spend more than eight months out of each year overseas, teaching and promoting karate worldwide. Amid this erratic and busy lifestyle, karate enables me to maintain a peaceful state of mind at all times. The lower abdomen, also called *hara* in Japanese, provides me with the basis for this ability.

But how is the lower abdomen—or *hara, seika-tanden*—strengthened through karate training? All of the basic techniques employed in karate, particularly such common techniques as the lunge punch and reverse punch, make use not only of the lower abdomen's muscular strength at the moment of impact, but also actively employ various internal forces: mental strength, spiritual strength, and visceral strength. When punching, all of the forces combine in a concerted effort and harmonize to produce explosive power. Accordingly, if the muscles in the lower abdomen are not being used, it is likely that incorrect training methods are being employed.

The question, however, still remains: Why does the lower abdomen serve such an important function? In short, it is because it represents the gravity center of the human body. While most people say that this is the body's "center," I use the term "gravity center" instead. The reason why is that, during a conversation with the mathematician Heisuke Hironaka I had used the word "center," and Mr. Hironaka emphatically responded, "Oh, you mean 'gravity center.'" I recall thinking that the term "gravity center" was more likely easier to understand.

Another reason the lower abdomen is of such importance is because training the *seika-tanden* and increasing abdominal muscle pressure produces a blood-cleansing process within the body.

I will discuss later in this book how karate students are first taught to employ breathing to focus power and concentration in the lower abdomen, and then to adapt their movements to their breathing.

The ability to focus power and concentration in the *seika-tanden* automatically leads to confidence and emotional stability. It is also reflected in such facets as attitude, character, and personality. For this reason, among warriors of the past, namely samurai, outstanding individuals who excelled in cultivating the literary arts while training in the military arts possessed character, courage, and a well-rounded personality. These people honed their skills with an emphasis on the *seika-tanden*.

In Buddhist *Zazen* meditation (a method of Zen training performed in a seated position), practitioners are also instructed to focus strength in the lower abdomen. Even when Japan's warrior class was entrusted with governing the country beginning in the Kamakura period (1185–1333), many of the samurai at the time, including the Shogun, took part in Zen training, placing great importance on the *seika-tanden* while working to cultivate character. For this reason, in Japan, such expressions as "achieving a *hara*" (*hara ga dekite iru*) and "having a well-set *hara*" (*hara ga suwatte iru*) are used in reference to broad-minded persons of character, individuals who are able to remain calm and collected in the face of any situation, and can deal with matters in a composed, level-headed manner.

A well-set *hara* enables a person to have confidence in his everyday life. And herein lies the allure of martial arts. The lower abdomen, depending on how it is combined with breathing and the way in which the body is used, can provide a feeling of encouragement in the face of unstable circumstances and, conversely, can have a calming effect during times of high tension. It is truly a profound phenomenon.

Due to the variety of movements employed in karate, concentrating power in the lower abdomen poses a challenge to beginning students and is particularly difficult for children. But when the hips unleash a powerful kick, it is the lower abdomen that ensures stability throughout the entire motion, from before the kick is delivered, to the instant that the kick makes contact, and finally the follow-through. It is for this reason that the lower abdomen represents the most important means of self-protection.

When instructing children, I often use an analogy to explain the fundamental principle of karate—namely that power originates from the lower abdomen, and techniques from the hips. I will tell them: "It's the same as with your fathers and mothers; if you think of your hips as being your father, then your lower abdomen is your mother. When your parents work together as a team, they create an outstanding household. In the same way, when your hips and lower abdomen work together as a team, you develop your body, your techniques, and your mind."

Training the lower abdomen improves the mind

From the time that I was a student, I have held my own thoughts about the *hara* and have continued my research in this field. Based on my own experiences, I would tell those around me that training the lower abdomen leads to improved intelligence. Responding to my ideas, my younger brother, who had just become a medical doctor, expressed concern, saying, "Big brother, while that may be true, people will laugh at you if you make such claims without any scientific proof to back them up. If I were you, I wouldn't go around telling people that."

Recently, however, that same brother came to me and, showing me a medical journal, said, "I can't believe it; what you said turned out to be true." He explained to me that it had been medically proven that, after life first appeared and over the course of human evolution, the nerve cells of the intestines and the nerve cells of the brain originally shared a very close relationship.

The role of the stomach is to digest food, and the intestine serves to absorb nutrients from the food we eat. The intestine, the largest of the body's immunological organs, is said to measure around seven meters (23 feet) in length and, if laid out flat, would cover the surface of a tennis court. Some 100 million nerve cells reside in the intestine, approximately one-half of the nerve cells located outside of the brain. Mankind has reached its present form following a lengthy evolution process, and the nerve cells of the intestinal canal and the nerve cells of the brain stem (which is responsible for our life-support functions and comprises the medulla oblongata, the midbrain, the pons, and the thalamus and hypothalamus) are essentially the same. A portion of the nerve cells from the intestinal canal migrated upward and achieved further development in the head, combining with the cerebrum to form the brain and facilitate human intelligence.

With regard to karate, I have received very interesting reports from many overseas instructors. They informed me that the school principals in each of these countries have expressed strong interest in karate, the reason being the realization that many of the students with the best grades practice karate.

Roughly ten years ago there was a noticeable increase in the number of children learning karate. And, not only in Japan but also in countries the world over, many educators were wondering why kids who practiced karate were getting such good grades, which led to the emergence of data highlighting the connection between karate and classroom performance. During the course of training in karate, the children learn about hierarchical relationships, decorum, and proper etiquette. And in the process, they learn to respect their parents. On top of that, their school performance improves as well.

The continued practice of karate not only leads to increased concentration but also serves as a form of intellectual training, since the nerve cells of the intestinal canal and those of the brain are essentially the same. Although I have heard that school principals have expressed doubt regarding this logic, to overseas instructors, I explain it this way: "Training the lower abdomen leads to greater concentration and endurance. And strengthening the *hara* also strengthens the mind."

The relationship of Yin (negative, dark, feminine) and Yang (positive, bright, masculine) is present in all things, and this also applies to the *hara*. We receive and absorb nutrition and calories from the food we eat, which enables us to grow. This is the outward role of the *hara*, the physical aspect, representing Yang qualities. On the opposite side, however, representing Ying, the *hara* serves a non-tangible role, a role that functions on the spiritual level. It is important to gain an understanding of this facet, and to train accordingly.

Students, company employees, and many other members of contemporary society have, over the course of their everyday lives, filled their heads with a great amount of information. They spend time gazing at computer screens and, in general, are exposed to a wide range of stimuli. As a result, they experience stiffness in their shoulders and lead very stressful lifestyles. For these people, practicing karate provides an opportunity to correct their posture, stretch their arms and legs, relieve the tension in their shoulders, and concentrate power in the abdomen, which helps to ward off illness and alleviate stress.

When people become mentally fatigued, they become irritable and lose the ability to effectively manage stress. While the role of the stomach is to digest food, one of the functions of the intestine is to digest all such emotional stress. This is why it is no surprise that karate training helps to overcome disease.

The path that is karate

Traditionally, martial arts (*budō* in Japanese), in Japan as well as karate's birthplace of Okinawa, began as a means of strengthening and building the mind and body. From there, they developed and gained widespread adoption. In other words, Japanese martial arts began with *kata* (forms) and etiquette. Take, for example, the Japanese arts of tea ceremony and flower arranging—while it is all right to drink the tea or arrange the flowers in any way that you may like, through the introduction of proper manners and etiquette, these art forms are identified in Japanese by the suffix *dō*, meaning path or way: *sa-dō* (literally "the way of tea") and *ka-dō* ("the way of flowers"). It is through *kata* and etiquette that these are recognized in terms of "a path," a path whose importance lies in understanding human nature, reflecting on yourself, and cultivating a mind that harmonizes with Mother Nature through a loving appreciation of flowers and nature. Other Japanese art forms that have been established as paths include *sho-dō* (the way of calligraphy) and *kō-dō* (the way of incense).

Attempting to learn such an art without embracing the path it entails, without attempting to acquire proper manners and etiquette, would result in the development of a character lacking in richness. It is for this very reason that Master Gichin Funakoshi, considered the father of modern karate, first attached the suffix *dō* to karate to form the word karate-dō.

While there are many strong, physically gifted sports athletes, there are some whose character gets called into question. These people, despite their physical strength, do not adhere to proper training methods that conform to the regulations and rules of their respective sports, but rather are only concerned with winning, with beating their opponents. With this single goal in mind, they tolerate practice and become physically stronger while they remain emotionally undeveloped. Such situations are very dangerous.

What is important to remember is that, without the proper frame of mind and practice methods based on sound training systems, there is the risk that students will move in the wrong directions. Depending on the sport, individuals with physical strength but a deficient attitude pose a real threat to those with lesser physical strength. Needless to say, if such men were to go in the streets looking for trouble, the results could be disastrous.

Under normal circumstances, people with the strength to conquer themselves—those whom we refer to as possessing tremendous inner strength—thrive on competition, which leads to self-confidence and a big heart, and, by extension, kindness to others. It is this kind of person who is truly strong, who does not feel the need for defiance or to flaunt his strength.

Karate training yields originality, flexible ways of thinking, and creative abilities. Strengthening the lower abdomen fosters a sense of greater emotional latitude, the flow of life energy, emotional breadth, and depth as an individual. It is said that young people today are prone to flying into fits of rage. This is due to a lack of emotional leeway and breadth in the abdominal region. When dissatisfaction, a rebellious spirit, and anger build up beyond what can be contained by the *hara*, it doesn't take much to push that person over the edge. With emotional latitude, however, when dissatisfaction mounts, it is possible, in a sense, to "expand" the abdomen—perhaps better referred to as the mind in this circumstance—enabling greater capacity. In this instance the *hara* only expands, so to speak, and does not break, which eliminates the risk of sudden fits of anger.

With greater breadth of character it becomes easier to see the big picture without dwelling on unimportant issues. This leads to the birth of flexible ideas. Take the artist, for example—breadth of character would allow that person to create highly imaginative artwork that is rich in creativity. The artist Hoan Kosugi, who progressed from oil painting to ink painting and was acclaimed as "the greatest modern artist of letters," studied karate under Master Gichin Funakoshi.

Training twice a week is the ideal schedule

This book comprises an intensive karate training course, describing a system which, if carried out continuously and with diligence over the course of one year, enables the attainment of black-belt-level proficiency. But before you begin practicing it is essential that you identify the goal that you aim to achieve. Perhaps your decision to begin studying karate was to pursue strength, or beauty—in any case, you must determine your own goal.

For those who want to become a black belt in one year, it is necessary for them to focus their energies and make a committed effort, setting aside one or two hours for training either every day or every other day.

If your aim is to get into shape and attain peace of mind through karate, then I would recommend taking an unhurried approach, dedicating two days a week to training. Through the additional peace of mind, you will be able to realize greater strength and richer affection.

Whatever the case may be, what is important is to continue training at your own pace, maintaining a schedule that conforms to your own personal rhythm. After all, power lies in perseverance.

There are people who diligently pursued karate while in school but, upon starting their adult life, quit because they felt that they had become too busy. If, however, you firmly make up your mind from the beginning to keep training, it is possible to avoid such outcomes. First and foremost, it is necessary to believe strongly that continued karate training will contribute to a long and healthy life, and will have a decidedly positive influence on your life. It is also essential that you make a firm commitment to continue practicing.

Among the people that train at my *dōjō*—Shotokan Karate International (SKI) Headquarters—there are more than a few middle-aged and older instructor-level students who have been practicing karate for a long time. Several of these students were members of their university karate teams some 30 or 40 years ago. These people come to train at my *dōjō* because, as instructors, it would not be appropriate for them to train at their own *dōjō*.

There are also many homemakers that attend my *dōjō*. Initially, these mothers came to enroll their children because they felt that their kids had become too much to handle; they felt incapable of satisfactorily disciplining and educating them. But when they saw the progressive changes that their children underwent, these women became curious as to the reason behind the improvement in attitude and decided to give karate a try themselves.

One fact that is a particular source of pride for me is that SKI instructors, both overseas and in Japan, remain active and healthy even into their late 60s.

Generally, people think that practicing karate is a tiring activity. They also believe that, as you get older, karate becomes no longer feasible. But karate practice demands nothing unreasonable. Furthermore, for people who find they tire easily, training two times per week represents the ideal level of exercise for relieving fatigue. If you exert yourself by training three or four times per week with the aim of increasing strength, the extra effort could lead to exhaustion, which can be alleviated through attitude, breathing methods, and movements designed to eliminate tiredness.

With the appropriate amount of karate training, it is possible to eliminate all forms of fatigue, including physical tiredness, muscle tension, cerebral exhaustion, and physical and mental lethargy. The ideal training menu involves practicing two times per week. If your aim is to maintain your health, then twice a week is the ideal amount; once a week is not enough.

The ideal full-body workout, combining muscle tension and relaxation

People who take martial arts training to extremes don't only firm up their bodies, they sometimes grow quite obstinate, getting hard heads as well. Therefore, in order to help relax this rigidity it is important to properly perform warm-up exercises before training, and cool-down exercises after. At the *dōjō*, due to a lack of time, I'm sorry to say that cool-down exercises are often neglected, which I believe is truly unfortunate. Ideally, training will begin with fifteen minutes of warm-up exercises, and conclude with seven to fifteen minutes of cool-down exercises.

For middle-aged and older students, it is best to practice basic karate techniques in a comfortably warm room for around 30 to 40 minutes. This will provide training for the *hara*. And, although we don't encounter many opportunities to work up a sweat as we get older, before long the perspiration will come flowing out from head to toe, and the feeling is better than almost anything else imaginable. It is more enjoyable than soaking in a hot spring or taking a sauna.

Lying down on Mother Earth and abandoning yourself to nature represents a horizontal form of harmony, while standing up straight, symbolized by the progress of plant growth, represents a vertical form of harmony: disciplined harmony. Karate employs movements and reactions that utilize these natural and physical laws. That is why the most important thing to keep in mind when training is to focus attention on the body's gravity center.

Basically, karate techniques are performed with good posture, moving while maintaining a perpendicular orientation to the floor. During this process a variety of movements are added, including moving forward and backward, to the left and right, bending, rotating, twisting, and leaping. A rule, however, which must be followed is that the body be perpendicular before and after these movements are launched. This will permit you to move freely and at will in any direction based on the circumstances at hand. Only when your gravity center is steadfastly under control does it become possible to carry out almost any movement without wavering.

Attaining harmony with yourself, with others, with the Earth

The training system employed in karate comprises three components: *kihon* (basics), *kumite* (sparring), and *kata* (form). Essentially, this book is intended as a self-study manual. But even when learning karate on your own, once a working understanding of the basics has been attained, it is essential to develop an awareness of an opponent, employing the imagination, concentration, and spirit to deliver punches capable of felling that opponent. Additionally, throughout the training system and techniques, special attention must be paid to maintaining harmony between the left and right sides of the body, harmony between the hands and feet, harmony between body movement and breathing, and balance and harmony between technique and power. Doing so will enable you, yourself, to automatically achieve a state of self-harmony.

The next step, *kumite*, because it involves the presence of a moving opponent, will provide you with the opportunity to learn how to harmonize with others by matching your movements, breathing, power, and techniques with those of your opponent. This leads to respecting, understanding, and getting along with an opponent, as well as improving personal relationships with others. Ultimately, it leads to and helps foster world peace. Accordingly, "technique" plays a role in all things.

The next step in the process requires that you envision, by yourself, a vast range of situations and scenes. As such, you will imagine yourself surrounded by enemies in every direction, and you will also imagine that you have become an enormous and towering presence in the universe wrapping your arms around the stars in the sky. With these grand visions, you will perform karate in midair. And by no means is it a difficult task to use your body in this way to express such a rich imagination, or such a big heart.

Once you are able to achieve harmony with yourself as well as with others, everything within the world generally falls into place. You will, however, become acutely aware of those who turn a blind eye to the problem of environmental pollution, thinking only of themselves while giving little consideration to the more important issue of protecting the future of our Earth. We must develop a greater love of nature, get along with nature, and cherish nature. The first step to achieving harmony with nature is to focus your gravity center in the *seika-tanden* and freely express your heart through your karate, maintaining a grand image in your mind. As you master each new technique, you will achieve harmony with yourself, with others, and with nature.

While there is no need for middle-aged and older students to take part in free sparring (*jiyū kumite*), one of the characteristics of promise sparring (*yakusoku kumite*) is that it enables such students to experience moderate levels of intensity. It is necessary for all people today to develop the fundamental awareness that it is dangerous to move sluggishly, to be caught unawares. Because people do not know what it means to be scared, they think nothing of heading directly toward oncoming cars while riding their bicycles around the city. Observing people in places like Tokyo, I am constantly amazed that so many people have reached such a state of vulnerability, and are so lacking in sensibility.

If human beings cannot employ their defensive instinct, they will be unable to quickly launch a proper response based on proper judgment in the event of a critical situation. Armed with this instinct in the face of, say, a tsunami, earthquake, or tropical storm, it is possible to immediately recognize the danger and take an appropriate course of action.

Promise sparring is an ideal means of training both the mind and the body to facilitate the functioning of this defensive instinct. Without repeatedly practicing face to face against an opponent, it is not possible to acquire the ability to exercise judgment and decisiveness. If you think, "Hmm . . . I wonder when I should make my move," then you will miss your opportunity to decide the match. Once your opponent drives in to deliver his attack, you must instantaneously take action. Such split-second exchanges of offensive and defensive techniques between attacker and defender represent the way in which promise sparring is meant to be practiced.

Even for someone with outstanding judgment, without the ability to make a necessary decision amid dangerous circumstances, that person will not be able to move into action. For example, upon the realization that a tsunami has struck, you may only survive if you act the very instant that you recognize the threat and the need to flee.

The role of free sparring is to develop an intuition capable of acutely detecting such dangers, as well as the courage to cope with adversity. For this reason, free sparring is a very important component of karate. Having said that, however, it is a skill that belongs to the realm of younger students, and I would prefer middle-aged and older students to focus on achieving greater peace of mind through karate. Most likely, for people in these age groups, attaining serenity represents one of the most important issues in today's bustling, stress-filled world.

There is a recognizable trait that characterizes people who want to learn karate. Of the many students who come to the karate *dōjō*, a relatively large number do not have outstanding athletic talent. Parents will bring their children in, saying that the kids lack coordination. And adults come to the *dōjō* because they are not good at sports. There are also many people who, believing that they are weak, come to train with the aim of becoming stronger. Some school students say that they want to learn karate to avoid being hit and made fun of by their classmates. They all become stronger.

I, too, wanted to get stronger by any possible means because I wanted to get revenge on a brute of a man who had given me a severe, unprovoked beating resulting in serious injuries when I was a young boy. I joined my university's karate team and endured the training, no matter how grueling it was, practicing twice as hard as everyone else and doing my best to make the karate techniques my own.

During the course of my karate training, however, I discovered a feeling welling inside me that enabled me to forgive this contemptible man, and my thirst for revenge simply faded away. While this is not something that can be proven with modern science, I believe that it does indicate the benefits of the training system, instruction, and various techniques that were being employed for karate at that time. I also received guidance from outstanding instructors and senior students. And, the fact that I was able to forgive the man whom I had detested for such a long time illustrates just how emotionally beneficial karate is—a phenomenon that I have experienced firsthand.

The ability to read your opponent's mind

There are some students who, although troublemakers in their youth, continue practicing karate from an early age. Because they also grow emotionally, when they meet someone who hasn't seen them for several years, they are often greeted by comments like: "You were such a little good-for-nothing. How did you grow into such a fine person?" This is a wonderful thing. In all of my experience—and not just through directly teaching in the karate *dōjō*, but in my travels while teaching around the world—I have yet to see or hear of any young person around me who practices karate that has turned out badly.

Among my adult students, there are those who are only able to come to the *dōjō* occasionally due to their busy work schedules. But even these students credit karate with giving them the ability to endure even the most trying of situations. Many of them also tell me that they can effectively manage difficult personal relationships, or that, even in the face of multiple difficulties, they are able to respond without panicking.

Whenever K, a university student, would compete in karate tournaments, he was constantly being rebuked by the referees, as he would soon lose his composure and become confrontational, getting into arguments with the referees. Upon graduating from university, this same young man began working for a real-estate firm, astonishing everyone around him with his exceptional sales results. By chance, I had the opportunity to meet with the chairman of the company, who explained K's performance by saying, "More than anything else, he has a fine character."

Additionally, I feel quite certain that K must have acquired what may be called a habit, or perhaps a faculty, which enabled him to read, to a degree, his opponents' minds. That is because in karate you practice matching your breathing, movements, power, and awareness with those of your opponent. In karate training, you first spend time carefully examining your opponent's movements. The instant your opponent tightens his muscles, you tighten yours; when he exhales, you exhale; and when he relaxes his muscles, you make your move and strike. This process is carried out repeatedly, but during this time, you watch your opponent's eyes.

Several months are spent in this way, practicing how to closely move in synchronization with an opponent. And by doing so, it becomes possible to read an opponent's thoughts merely by looking into his eyes. This is not something that can be explained by reason, but rather something that can only be understood and acquired through karate experience and practice.

I would like to share with you an additional truth that also cannot be explained scientifically. One thing I make a habit of teaching is that when facing an opponent who is senior in level, look at only one of his eyes with both of yours. Because he has more experience and is strong, if you take in both of his eyes, it is easy to feel overwhelmed—like a frog being challenged by a snake—making it difficult to gain any benefit out of training. But, by using both of your eyes to look at only one of your opponent's eyes, it is possible to minimize the element of fear. This will become one source of psychological energy that will enable you to catch up to senior students.

Also, while it may be viewed as non-scientific, it is my theory that, when discussing matters of importance with someone, you must always face that person so that your navel points in his direction. Doing so will facilitate the flow of your spiritual energy to him and, should your energy be sufficiently strong, will enable you to take in his energy as well. This approach will lead to productive discussions and successful negotiations.

I tell people that, if they don't believe this theory, then they should try it for themselves. To students attending school, I say, "If you have a favor to ask of your teacher, or something that needs to be taken care of at your school, then stand with your belly button facing the teacher when you speak." I tell them that if they do that, their teachers will understand what they are saying, comply, and give them the help that they need. And sure enough, before long, several of the kids come back to me and say, "Kanazawa-sensei! It really works. I did what you said and talked to my teacher with my belly button facing her, and everything went perfectly!"

I am not certain of the reason behind this phenomenon, but I believe it likely that, by pointing your navel in the direction of the person to whom you are speaking, your gravity center and lower abdomen are able to resonate with those of that person, enabling each other's energy to merge.

As is evident from all of this, there are still many, many things about the human body that mankind has yet to understand. While each individual human being is a small cosmos unto his or her self, within the space of the grand cosmos, and within the realm of the small human cosmos, there still remain countless wonders that we are not able to explain through modern science. And by no means is the space to which I refer empty; it is a space from which all things come into being, a space filled with anything and everything, yielding various forms of energy that spills out and flows forth. This is the philosophical meaning contained within the initial Chinese character used to write karate (空手), which is also used to write the Japanese word for space (空間, pronounced *kūkan*).

The Milky Way galaxy, one of the more than 200 billion galaxies that make up the universe, contains between 200 and 400 billion fixed stars. A small planet, Earth, orbits one of these stars within our Solar System, and it is on this planet that we live, along with more than six billion people. While we are a minuscule existence when viewed from outer space, the 60 trillion cells that make up the human body, including the 14 billion cells comprising the brain, which is capable of contemplating this infinite universe, possess truly remarkable powers.

Thinking in these terms, we cannot simply dismiss these phenomena by saying that we do not understand them, or that they are based on lies. In fact, there are many people who understand them to be true, as these people are capable of sensing such powers on a physical level.

Karate fosters strong individuals with merciful hearts, courage, and a sense of justice

More than anything else, I would like for you to use this amazing martial art of karate as a means of becoming aware of your true self, improving your character, and developing your abilities. If you have completed your schooling and are now out in the world, I would like you to draw on karate in your daily life to perform well in your work, to be a good member of society and a good citizen.

Assuming that I had 100 students, rather than working to raise 10 outstanding karate athletes, my aim would be to teach all 100 to improve themselves as individuals. I am not interested in karate that only trains students into superior athletes, but in karate that develops people as useful members of society.

The ultimate goal of my karate instruction is world peace. The only way to achieve true world peace is by producing as many people as possible with merciful hearts, courage, and a sense of justice. In other words, producing as many true leaders as possible. The ability to remain level-headed in the face of any occurrence, to which I referred at the beginning of this preface, is an absolute must for any budding leader entrusted with creating the future.

But the heart of a leader is not something that can be developed overnight; it needs to be nurtured gradually, in steps. To achieve this goal, it must be understood that a sense of justice, courage, confidence, and the ability to take action, as well as the framework of karate techniques and the associated training system, are the steps to improving oneself as a human being.

Physical exercise is but one path, which should be combined with moral education and intellectual training. Without the body, virtue and intellect do not exist. The body, the soul, the mind, virtue, and intellect are not unrelated components, but rather blend harmoniously together, and karate-dō is an effective training system which aspires to improve and deepen one's character to realize a more complete individual.

This book explains how to use the *hara* and provides an entire step-by-step approach to becoming a black belt in karate, beginning with the loosening of the muscles in preparation for training, through to the coordination of breathing. Additionally, for particularly ardent students, I have also included technical applications for many of the techniques that are introduced.

For this reason, this book is not intended only for beginning learners of karate, but also offers something of value to intermediate and advanced students. People have a tendency to believe that if they are able to do a thing once, then they will always be able to do it, even without regular practice. From the perspective of an instructor, however, once you start teaching karate and begin noticing the improvement in your students' skills, you quickly feel the need to relearn the basics and often find yourself dedicating your time to training once again in this area. Additionally, as you read this book, I think you may discover more than a few facets of karate training that you had not been aware of, or had overlooked.

Something else that I would like everyone who reads this book to understand and to put into practice is the first of Master Gichin Funakoshi's twenty precepts of karate, which states: Do not forget that karate begins with a bow, and ends with a bow. While bowing from the traditional Japanese style of sitting, with the legs folded underneath, is a means of displaying gratitude and respect, some people may find it unacceptable to lower their heads in this way due to their religious beliefs. I would like to stress, however, that karate is a part of Japanese culture, and it is important to accept it as Japanese culture. Having a *dōjō* enables us to practice karate, as does the presence of training partners. We must be thankful for this. And to demonstrate that appreciation, we kneel and bow our heads deeply at the beginning and end of training.

There are some people who make it as far as giving karate a try, but soon quit, believing that it is not for them. If you have just begun training, or have decided that you would like to learn karate-dō, then I would like to encourage you to continue training so that you can experience for yourself the appeal that karate holds.

Even if you have trouble understanding what you are doing, please do not simply give up because you think you have no aptitude for karate. At the very least, give yourself one year to continue training and see what happens. While it is a wonderful thing to be able to understand and acquire karate techniques quickly, by spending more time and learning them gradually, you gain the advantage of a deeper, more comprehensive understanding. And, with continued training in this way, following a training approach that suits you personally, I feel certain that, before long, you will become aware of a significant transformation in both mind and body. And even if your karate experience should end after only a brief duration, at some point in the future the time will come when that experience will prove beneficial. That is because you have had a taste of the spirit, the techniques, and the philosophy of karate-dō.

The path that is Karate-dō

For anyone starting down the path of karate, the desire to become strong is very important. Without this desire, not only will the pursuit be given up easily, but developing proper technical skills will become difficult, individual techniques will lack conviction, and training will offer only physical exercise, resulting in nothing more than a recreational activity.

Karate is, above everything else, a martial art. As such, training in karate entails a great degree of severity for all who study it.

During the first stage of training the most important thing is to focus every ounce of energy and effort on the basics. Practicing the basics time and again will lead naturally to the development of a feel for karate-dō and will gradually infuse spirit into the techniques.

The path of martial arts, like the path to knowledge, offers no convenient shortcuts. Unlike knowledge, however, learning karate is, initially, a physical pursuit, not a mental one. If this were not the case, then the pursuit would lack any practical value. Without intense training, involving pushing the body to its limits, true mastery of karate is not possible. That is why maintaining a single-minded desire to become strong is of such importance.

Forever focusing simply on becoming strong, however, results in techniques that lack heart and eventually become little more than a sideshow as all semblance of dignity fades away. If the sole aim involves nothing more than knocking down one's opponent, then it is not necessary to practice karate since there are plenty of easier ways to achieve such a goal.

While involving a greater degree of difficulty, contests of karate-dō attach importance to the beauty and style with which an opponent is defeated. Rather than trying to win at any cost, the value of fair play must be thoroughly ingrained, which will, in turn, have a positive influence on the techniques themselves. In other words, the mind and the technique become one. Complement this with a sufficient amount of diligent training and victory in competition is certain to follow.

Additionally, to enable original thoughts and opinions that you can call your own, academic study aimed at cultivating the mind must not be ignored. Granted, pursuit of the dual paths of the literary and martial arts is no easy task, but even the effort of trying to attain this goal will open up opportunities that would otherwise not avail themselves. Even the most intense of battles will not end in defeat.

Such investments are sure to pay dividends at some later stage in the lives of all who pursue the path of karate.

Dōjō-kun (Code of ethics)

1. Seek perfection of character
2. Be faithful
3. Endeavor
4. Respect others
5. Refrain from violent behavior

Before presenting the lessons contained in this book, I believe it is important first to review such basics as the correct names and functions of the various techniques, stances, and body parts most commonly employed in karate.

Please study the photographs and explanations in this section carefully to ensure a sufficient understanding of these fundamentals prior to practicing the exercises that follow.

KARATE
The fundamentals

USING THE HANDS AND FEET

1. Hands and arms

The correct way to make a fist

Being able to make a fist (*kobushi* in Japanese) properly and quickly is critical in karate. Doing so will help prevent sprained fingers and other hand injuries.

1) Extend and align the index, middle, ring, and little fingers.

2) Bend the four fingers inward, beginning with the little finger, followed by each adjoining finger.

3) Fold the fingers inward until the fingertips touch the base of the fingers.

4) Continue curling the four fingers inward, tightly folding them into the palm.

5) Fold the thumb down so that it presses firmly on the index and middle fingers. The thumb and little finger press tightly against the fingers in between to form a strong fist.

Beginning students tend to focus only on keeping the thumb firmly in place, resulting in a fist that lacks proper balance. Accordingly, care must be taken to make sure that the little finger is also tightly folded and pressing against the neighboring fingers.

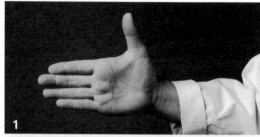
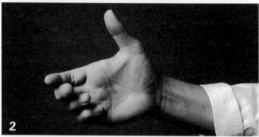

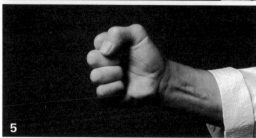

Seiken (Fore fist)

Seiken is the most commonly used fist in karate punches. For this reason, frequent practice is essential to ensure that it is formed properly.

In *seiken* the first knuckles of the index and middle fingers are used to strike the target. The wrist is kept straight so that the back of the hand and the top of the wrist describe a straight line, enabling the full energy of a punch to be concentrated in the front of the fist at the location of the first two knuckles. The wrist must be kept rigid and straight at all times; a bent wrist when punching could result in injury.

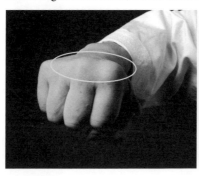 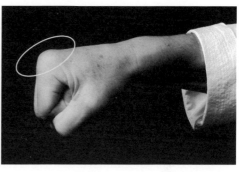

Uraken (Back fist)

Uraken, formed in the same manner as *seiken*, can be used for strikes to the face and the side of the body. The back of the hand, around the first knuckles of the index and middle fingers, is used to strike the target. To deliver a powerful *uraken* strike, the arm is

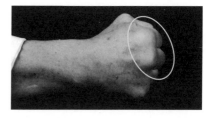

used like a whip, with a snapping motion at the elbow. Without the snap of the elbow, an *uraken* strike will lose its effectiveness.

Tettsui (Hammer fist)

T*ettsui*, also formed in the same manner as *seiken*, can be used for strikes to the head and body. The base of the fist is used to strike the target and, like *uraken*, its effectiveness relies on the snap of the elbow.

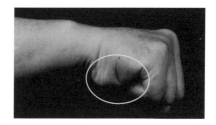

Ippon-ken (One-knuckle fist)

Ippon-ken is similar to *seiken* except that the second knuckle joint of the index finger protrudes, with the bent index finger tightly sandwiched between the flat of the thumb and the middle finger. The protruding knuckle of the index finger is used to strike such vulnerable points as the bridge of the nose and the area just below the nose, making *ippon-ken* a highly effective weapon.

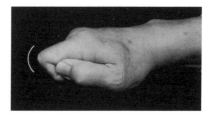

Nakadaka Ippon-ken (Middle-finger one-knuckle fist)

Nakadaka ippon-ken is formed in the same way as *seiken* except that the first knuckle joint of the middle finger protrudes. The protruding knuckle is used to strike the target in the same way as *ippon-ken*.

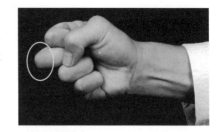

Hiraken (Fore-knuckle fist)

Hiraken is formed by folding the index, middle, ring, and little fingers so that the tips of the fingers touch the edge of the palm behind the first knuckles. The flat of the thumb presses against the side of the index finger. *Hiraken* can be used in attacks to such vulnerable points as the area just below the nose.

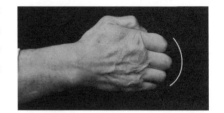

Yokoken (Side fist)

In *yokoken*, which is formed in the same way as *ippon-ken*, the second knuckle joint of the thumb is used to strike the target. It is effective for attacks directed at such vulnerable points as the temple.

Nukite (Spear hand)

While the term *nukite* is commonly used to refer to *shihon* (four-finger) *nukite*, there are other types of *nukite* as well: *nihon* (two-finger) *nukite* and *ippon* (one-finger) *nukite*. Since the fingertips are used to strike the target, they are subject to a tremendous amount of stress. To prevent sprains and other possible injuries, strengthening the fingers by regularly thrusting them into sand or rice is recommended.

Shihon-nukite (Four-finger spear hand)

In *shihon-nukite* the index, middle, ring, and little fingers are aligned and extended. The four fingers are bent slightly and the thumb is tightly locked against the edge of the hand. *Shihon-nukite* can be used for strikes to the solar plexus and the side of the body.

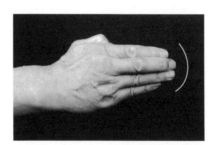

Nihon-nukite (Two-finger spear hand)

In *nihon-nukite*, which can be used for strikes targeting the eyes and nose, the index and middle fingers are extended and bent slightly.

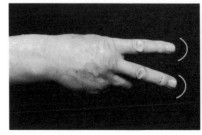

Ippon-nukite (One-finger spear hand)

To form *ippon-nukite* the index finger is extended and bent slightly while the middle, index, and little fingers are tightly folded back as in *hiraken*. The index finger is tightly sandwiched between the locked thumb and the middle finger. *Ippon-nukite* can be used for attacks directed at such vulnerable points as the eyes.

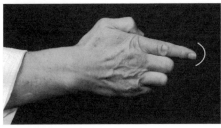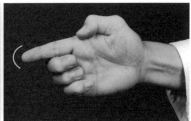

Shutō (Knife hand)

In *shutō* the outer edge of the hand below the little finger is used like a sword for blocking and attacking. The index, middle, ring, and little fingers are aligned and extended while the thumb is tightly locked against the edge of the hand.

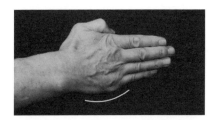

Haitō (Ridge hand)

In *haitō* the inner edge of the hand around the first knuckle of the index finger is used like a sword for blocking and attacking. Compared with *shutō*, the thumb is pulled further inward toward the palm.

Seiryūtō (Ox-jaw hand)

In *seiryūtō* the outer edge of the hand near the wrist strikes the target. The wrist is bent back as the lower edge of the hand is thrust out sharply to block or attack.

Teishō (Palm heel)

Teishō is formed by bending the wrist upward and pushing the heel of the hand forward. The heel is thrust forward sharply for attacks to the chin and elsewhere, as well as for blocking.

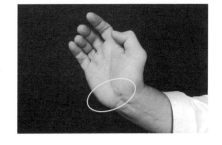

Keitō (Chicken-head wrist)

In *keitō* the base and first knuckle of the thumb are used for strikes aimed at the armpit or the punching arm. The hand is bent downward at the wrist so that the base of the thumb is in line with the thumb side of the forearm.

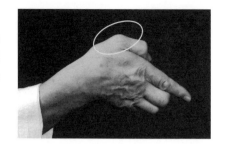

Kakutō (Bent wrist)

In *kakutō* the wrist is bent downward and the top of the wrist is used for striking the target. *Kakutō* is highly effective in strikes to the chin.

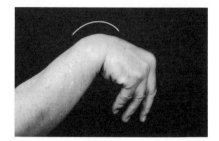

Washide (Eagle hand)

In *washide* the tips of all five fingers are pinched together to form a point, similar in appearance to a bird's beak, used for attacks to such vulnerable points as the throat and the temple. While an effective attack, care must be taken to prevent sprained fingers and other injuries.

Kumade (Bear hand)

In *kumade*, formed by folding the fingers and thumb so the fingertips just touch the edge of the palm, the palm is used to strike the target. The palm is thrust out sharply, making *kumade* an effective weapon for strikes to the face.

Ude (Arm)

Most of the basic blocking techniques employed in karate are performed using the arms. The forearm, almost all of which can be used for blocking, is divided into four basic lengthwise regions: *uchi-ude* (inner arm), the thumb side of the forearm;

soto-ude (outer arm), the little-finger side of the forearm; *haiwan* (back arm), the posterior surface of the forearm leading into the back of the hand; and *fukuwan* ("belly" arm), the anterior surface of the forearm leading into the palm.

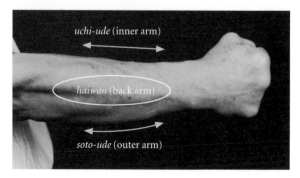

uchi-ude (inner arm)

haiwan (back arm)

soto-ude (outer arm)

Empi (Elbow)

When facing an opponent at close range, the elbow can be used as an effective weapon for strikes to the face, chin, solar plexus, and the side of the body. The elbow is also well suited for use in self-defense applications.

2. Feet and legs

Hiza (Knee)

The knee can be used at close range for strikes to the face, side of the body and groin. It can also be used for self defense by women, children, and people lacking in physical strength.

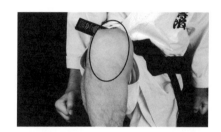

Koshi (Ball of the foot)

In karate, the ball of the foot is most frequently used when delivering kicks. With the toes curled upward, the ball of the foot can be used to attack almost any part of the body, including the chin, chest, abdomen, and groin.

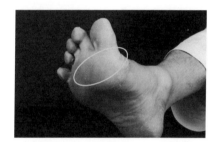

Sokutō (Foot edge)

Used in side kicks, *sokutō* makes use of the outer edge of the foot. The foot is bent inward at the ankle and firmly locked in place.

Haisoku (Instep)

In *haisoku* the top of the foot, from the ankle to above the toes, is used as the striking surface. The foot is extended downward and the toes are bent down. The area around the top of the toes is called *jōhaisoku*.

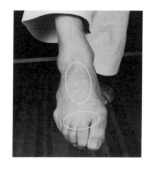

Sokusō (Tips of toes)

In *sokusō* all of the toes are clustered together and the ends of the toes are used to strike the target.

Kakato (Heel)

The heel of the foot is used in back kicks.

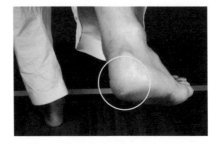

Sokutei (Sole)

The sole of the foot is mainly used for blocking.

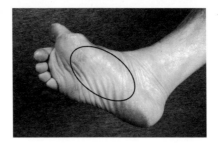

Stances

The expression *ichigeki hissatsu* (to kill with a single strike) is frequently associated with karate. This is because karate attacks utilize the concentration of power to generate tremendous destructive force. Accordingly, stances that are not performed properly do not permit power to be sufficiently focused, which reduces the level of destructive force produced and leaves the body unprepared for the reaction that accompanies an attack.

Also, when defending against attacks of great destructive power, blocking techniques may prove inadequate without a solid stance.

The importance of proper stances in karate is not limited to the technical considerations mentioned above. Maintaining a proper stance also offers health-related benefits: pushing the spine's fifth thoracic vertebra and the third lumbar vertebra forward provides the same beneficial effects as acupressure (*shiatsu*).

In the explanations that follow, the weight distributions given are intended only as a basic guide. Actual weight distributions may differ depending on individual body type or other physical traits.

1. Shizentai (Natural posture)

Shizentai refers to stances that can be assumed naturally and with ease, but facilitate the execution of subsequent movements. Although referred to as natural stances, the back should be extended and straight with the feeling of pushing the crown of the head upward, and care must be taken to prevent any unnecessary tension.

a) **Heisoku-dachi**
   (Closed parallel stance)

The feet are closed and aligned so that they touch each other.

b) **Musubi-dachi**
   (Closed V stance)

The heels touch each other with the toes pointing outward so that the feet describe the letter V. This is the stance used when standing at attention (*ki-o-tsuke*).

c) **Soto hachiji-dachi**
   (Open V stance)

The heels are placed approximately shoulder-width apart with the toes pointing outward at an angle.

d) **Heikō-dachi**
   (Open parallel stance)

The heels are placed approximately shoulder-width apart with the toes pointing straight ahead so that the feet are parallel to each other.

e) **Renoji-dachi**
   (L stance)

The heel of the rear foot is turned outward at an angle while the front foot, which is placed roughly one foot's length ahead of the rear foot, points straight ahead. A straight line extending forward along the floor would touch the heel of the rear foot and pass underneath the front foot.

2. Neko ashi-dachi (Cat stance)

In *neko ashi-dachi* the rear leg supports 90 percent of the body's weight. The rear foot is turned outward at an angle and the back knee is bent sharply. A straight line extending forward on the floor directly underneath the body would touch the heel of the rear foot and pass underneath the front foot, which is located about one foot's length in front of the rear foot. There are two possible variations for positioning the front foot: with the tips of the toes lightly touching the floor, or with the ball of the foot resting on the floor. Additionally, both knees can be tightly drawn inward in a defensive posture, or can remain in a position enabling an attack. As there is a tendency to slouch when practicing *neko ashi-dachi*, it is important to remember to keep the back straight.

3. Sanchin-dachi (Hourglass stance)

The heels are placed approximately shoulder-width apart with the front foot turned inward at a 45-degree angle and the rear foot pointing straight ahead. A straight line extending sideways on the floor directly underneath the body would touch the back of the heel of the front foot and the tip of the big toe of the rear foot. Both knees are bent and drawn inward tightly. To ensure a proper stance, it is also important to tighten the anus.

4. Zenkutsu-dachi (Front stance)

When viewed from the front, the feet are shoulder-width apart. When viewed from the side, the distance between the front foot and rear foot is double the width of the shoulders. The front foot faces forward and is turned inward slightly so that the outer edge of the foot describes a line pointing straight ahead. The front knee is bent sharply and pressure is applied outward to keep the knee firmly in place. The rear leg is extended fully and the rear foot points outward at about a 45-degree angle. The front leg supports 60 percent of the body's weight and the rear leg 40 percent. Beginning students have a tendency to reduce the width of the stance, standing so the front foot is nearly in line with the rear foot when viewed from the front, which results in a stance that lacks stability.

5. Kōkutsu-dachi (Back stance)

The distance between the front foot and rear foot is double the width of the shoulders. When viewed from the front, the heel of the front foot is aligned with the heel of the rear foot. The outer edge of the rear foot forms a right angle to the line described by the heels of the feet. The rear knee is bent sharply with pressure applied outward. The front foot faces forward and is turned inward slightly so that the outer edge of the foot describes a line pointing straight ahead. The front knee is extended but bent slightly with pressure applied outward. The hips are kept low and energy is focused in the lower abdomen with the feeling of sitting in a chair. The rear leg supports 70 percent of the body's weight while the front leg supports the remaining 30 percent.

6. Fudō-dachi (Rooted stance)

When viewed from the front, the feet are a little more than shoulder-width apart. When viewed from the side, the distance between the front foot and rear foot is double the width of the shoulders. Both knees are bent with the feet parallel to each other and pointing at a 45-degree angle relative to the front. The center of gravity is focused slightly forward of center so that the front leg supports 55 percent of the body's weight and the rear leg 45 percent.

7. Hangetsu-dachi (Half-moon stance)

When viewed from the front, the feet are shoulder-width apart. When viewed from the side, the distance between the front foot and rear foot is a little less than double the width of the shoulders. The front foot is turned inward at a 45-degree angle and the rear foot points outward at a 45-degree angle. Both knees are drawn inward as if being pulled together. The anus must also be tightened to prevent the backside from sticking out.

8. Kiba-dachi (Straddle-leg stance)

The distance between the feet is double the width of the shoulders. Both feet face forward and are turned inward slightly so that the outer edges of the feet are almost parallel. Both knees are bent with pressure applied outward to keep them firmly in place. To ensure a strong stance, it is also important to tighten the muscles of the abdomen and buttocks. *Kiba-dachi* represents the foundation on which all karate stances are based.

9. Shiko-dachi (Square stance)

The distance between the feet is double the width of the shoulders. Both feet are turned outward at an angle and both knees are bent with pressure applied outward to keep them firmly in place. As in *kiba-dachi*, it is important to tighten the muscles of the abdomen and buttocks to ensure a strong stance.

BREATHING TECHNIQUES FOR KARATE

It goes without saying that breathing is an essential part of living. The act of inhaling and exhaling is something that most of us probably do without even thinking.

Practice breathing a few times each day while paying attention to the following points:

- Maintain good posture with the back straight and extended
- Relax all of the muscles in the body
- Breathe in through the nose and exhale strongly but calmly through the mouth
- After completely exhaling, hold the breath, but not to the point where it becomes uncomfortable
- Inhale slowly and deeply down into the lower abdomen (called *tanden*, located roughly eight centimeters [a little over three inches] below the navel)
- After inhaling, hold the breath, but not to the point where it becomes uncomfortable
- Continue breathing in the same manner

Karate makes use of abdominal breathing, which is based on the points listed above. The duration of an inhalation or exhalation employed in karate will vary depending on the technique being used. Also, when launching techniques, inhaling and exhaling is constrained to roughly the 80-percent point, which enables movements to be performed smoothly and is essential for maximizing speed and power. Breathing in this manner also enhances mental energy.

Exhaling through the nose results in power focused in the upper abdomen while exhaling through the mouth permits power to be concentrated in the lower abdomen. Accordingly, in karate, it is essential to breathe out through the mouth.

Here are several of the most common breathing patterns employed in karate:
1) Long exhalation-Long inhalation
2) Short exhalation-Short inhalation
3) Long exhalation-Short inhalation
4) Short exhalation-Long inhalation
5) Long inhalation-Short divided exhalations
6) Short inhalation-Short divided exhalations
Which breathing pattern is used depends on the type of movement or techniques being performed. For example:

1) Straight punch (*Choku-zuki*)
Breathe out while delivering the punch, hold the breath during the moment of impact, and then breathe in while relaxing the muscles. (Long exhalation-Short inhalation)

2) Front snap kick (*Mae-geri*)
Breathe out during the kick and withdrawal of the foot, and then breathe in while returning the kicking foot to the floor. (Long exhalation-Short inhalation)

3) Back-fist strike (*Uraken-uchi*)
Like the front snap kick, the back-fist strike employs a snapping motion, generated from the elbow. Breathe out during the strike and withdrawal of the fist, and then breathe in normally. (Long exhalation-Regular inhalation)

4) Lunge punch (*Oi-zuki*)
Breathe in during the initial three-quarters of the step toward the target, and then breathe out in a single burst at the moment of impact as the step is completed. (Long inhalation-Long exhalation)

5) Inside-to-outside block (*Uchi ude-uke*) while stepping forward
Like the lunge punch, inhale through the initial three-quarters of the step, up to the point where the blocking hand is drawn beneath the underarm on the opposite side of the body, and then, during the last quarter step, exhale at the instant that the stepping foot is planted and the block is executed. (Long inhalation-Long exhalation)

6) Three-punch combination (*Sanbon-zuki*) while stepping forward
Inhale during the initial three-quarters of the step, and breathe out during the remainder of the step in segmented exhalations while executing the three successive punches. The duration of the first exhalation is slightly longer than the two subsequent exhalations. (Long inhalation-Short divided exhalations)

7) Reverse punch (*Gyaku-zuki*) while standing in place
When performed in two counts, breathe out during the delivery of the reverse punch and breathe in slowly while returning to the ready position. (Long exhalation-Long inhalation)

When the two-step sequence (the punch and the return to the ready position) is performed in one count, breathe out in succession during each of the two actions. (Long divided exhalations)

It should be noted that the use of the expression "long" to describe exhalations and inhalations does not always refer to length in terms of time. The actual length of each breath depends on the type of karate technique being performed and, as such, can only be described in relative terms.

While it may seem difficult to get the knack of proper breathing at first, by keeping the concepts in mind while practicing, the process will gradually become second nature over time.

Although the points presented here are potentially fatal areas of vulnerability, as they are pressure points, they can also be used to realize therapeutic benefits. A periodic review of these illustrations is recommended to gain familiarity with these points on the body.

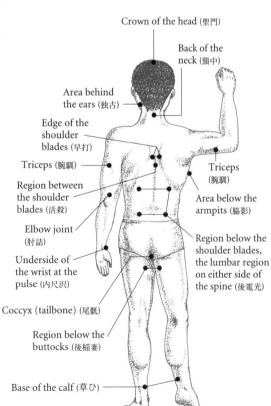

Area above and below the eyes (晴曇)

Crown of the head (聖門)

Area between the crown and forehead (天倒)

Underside of the wrist at the pulse (内尺沢)

Temples (霞)

Bridge of the nose (烏兎)

Eyes (眼星)

Region below the nose (人中)

Area below the lower lip (下昆)

Jaw (三日月)

Side of the neck (松風)

Elbow joint (肘詰)

Collar bone (村雨)

Base of the sternum (胸尖)

Adam's apple (秘中)

Sternum (膻中)

Area below the armpits (脇影)

Triceps (腕馴)

Solar plexus (水月)

Region below the nipples (雁下)

Region between the seventh and eighth ribs (電光)

Region below the navel (明星)

Side of the body above the hips (稲妻)

Back of the wrist (外尺沢)

Testicles (金的)

Back of the hand (手甲)

Inside of upper thighs (夜光)

Lower thighs (伏兎)

Inside region of the ankle (内踝)

Shins (向骨)

Instep (甲利)

Outside edge of the instep (草隠)

Crown of the head (聖門)

Back of the neck (頸中)

Area behind the ears (独古)

Edge of the shoulder blades (早打)

Triceps (腕馴)

Triceps (腕馴)

Region between the shoulder blades (活殺)

Area below the armpits (脇影)

Elbow joint (肘詰)

Region below the shoulder blades, the lumbar region on either side of the spine (後電光)

Underside of the wrist at the pulse (内尺沢)

Coccyx (tailbone) (尾骶)

Region below the buttocks (後稲妻)

Base of the calf (草ひ)

Breathing routine following each series of techniques

The following breathing exercise should be performed upon returning to a natural-posture open V stance after practicing a technique or series of techniques. The routine serves to supply a rich supply of oxygen to the blood, which aids the muscles in functioning properly and reduces the risk of muscle stiffness and possible muscle damage.

1) After completing the final technique, return to an open V stance while extending both arms downward in front of the body, crossing them at the wrists for an instant before pulling the elbows straight back, drawing the fists alongside the hips with the backs of the hands facing outward. While pulling the elbows back, expand the chest and inhale deeply through the nose, keeping the lower abdomen relaxed.

2) Upon inhaling fully, slowly drive the fists downward in front of the thighs, steadily exhaling through the mouth while contracting the chest and tightening the abdominal muscles.

3) After exhaling fully, unclench the fists and begin inhaling again through the nose, relaxing the hands while bringing them up beside the hips and then downward again just behind the buttocks. Press the hands downward with the palms facing the floor and the fingers directed toward the front, as if resting the hands on the edge of a tabletop positioned directly behind you. While pushing downward with the hands, push the crown of the head up toward the ceiling, rising on the balls of the feet while stretching the entire body.

4) After inhaling to the limit, exhale once again through the mouth and relax the entire body while lowering the heels and forming the hands into fists, returning to the original natural-posture stance with the arms extended downward in front of the body.

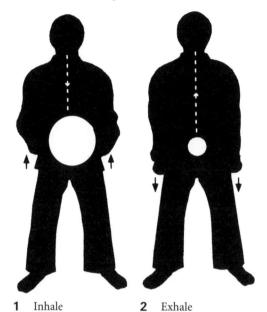

1 Inhale   **2** Exhale

3 Inhale   **4** Exhale

All inhalations must be performed through the nose and all exhalations through the mouth.

Mokusō (Silent meditation)

Mokusō, or silent meditation, is usually performed at the start and end of each training session for around one minute to calm the mind and relax the body.

Mokusō is performed while sitting *seiza*-style (kneeling with the legs folded underneath, the buttocks resting on the heels, and the tops of the feet against the floor) with the hands resting palms down on the upper thighs. The back is kept straight and extended with the nose positioned in line with the navel and the eyes half open, focused on a point on the floor approximately 45 centimeters (18 inches) in front of the knees.

Inhale slowly through the nose, envisioning the breath traveling up to the forehead, across the crown of the head and down the back of the skull and spine toward the anus. Imagine the breath collecting in the *hara* (lower abdomen), winding into ever smaller circles until disappearing into a minuscule point. Then begin to exhale slowly, concentrating on the breath as it emerges from a single point in the *hara* and gradually winds outward, traveling upward towards the navel, through the solar plexus and throat, and finally out of the mouth. Keep the abdomen relaxed when breathing in, and gently contract it when breathing out.

For most beginners, a single complete breathing cycle (inhalation and exhalation) should take about 15 seconds. More advanced students should perform a single cycle in around 20 seconds. These times, however, are merely intended as general guidelines; individual students may require more or less time to complete a breathing cycle.

Over time, through *mokusō*, students will learn to control the ebb and flow of their emotions. This will enable them to get into the proper frame of mind prior to training, and to relax both the mind and the body following a workout.

Inhale

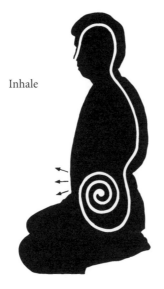

Exhale

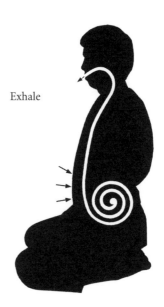

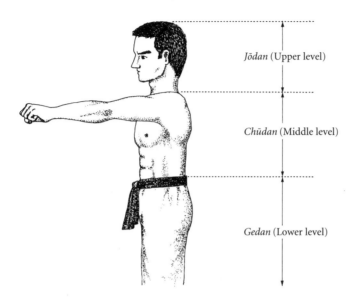

Jōdan (Upper level)

Chūdan (Middle level)

Gedan (Lower level)

How to train using this book

The course outlined in this book assumes individual training sessions of two hours per day, three days per week (with each training day followed by a day of rest). As such, almost anyone should be able to keep pace without much difficulty.

At the beginning of each training session it is essential to perform the warm-up exercises described in the first lesson of Chapter 1 for about 20 minutes to limber up the body. Also, as you progress through the book, it is advisable to review the lessons from the previous training session and the previous week before starting each new lesson. In karate, as in all sports, the quickest means to improvement is through repeated practice.

While at first you may not be able to perform the exercises in the same way as shown in the photographs, including the warm-up exercises, it will become possible through repeated and regular practice. Additionally, for all of the basic exercises, it is important to gradually increase the speed with which you perform them.

And finally, although the technical explanations presented in this book are given for one side of the body only (for example, using the right hand to deliver a reverse punch), it is necessary to practice all techniques using both sides. Practicing with the weaker arm and leg is particularly important to ensure a proper balance between the left and right sides of the body.

空手

CHAPTER I

Basic Techniques

- Warm-up exercises (Approx. 20 min.)
- Punching fundamentals
- Mae-geri (Front snap kick) 1

Warm-up exercises 準備体操

Since karate demands the sudden application and release of power, as well as the rapid flexion and extension of various joints, it is essential to warm up the body prior to training. When performing the following warm-up exercises, it is important to be aware of which parts of the body are being used, and to breathe in accordance with each movement. Also, sufficient time should be taken to ensure that each exercise is performed properly.

Stimulating the body prior to strenuous physical activity promotes the circulation of energy, blood, and body heat, which awakens mental energy and helps to prevent the occurrence of injuries during training. It also contributes to the burning of fat. Although warm-up exercises may be viewed by some as an inconvenience, training should always begin with a proper warm-up routine.

1) Light jumping

In accordance with one of the cardinal rules of physical exercise, which states that exercise should begin with the part of the body farthest away from the heart, and because of the large number of muscles and capillaries in the soles of the feet, warm-up exercises should always begin with light jumping in place. Because jumping is a weight-bearing exercise, it contributes to the building of strong bones and prevents calcium loss.

2) Neck exercises

These exercises provide stimulation to the neck, which supports the weight of the head.

a. Forward and backward

b. Tilting side to side

c. Turning side to side

d. Neck rolls

3) Arm exercises

3) Arm exercises (Forward and backward, eight times in each direction)

When rotating the arms forward, exhale when tensing the muscles and inhale naturally. When rotating the arms backward, inhale when tensing the muscles and exhale naturally.

4) Upper body stretch: Side-to-side

Bend at the waist to the left and then to the right to stretch the muscles along the side of the body. Alternate sides, stretching four times to each side.

5) Upper body stretch: Forward and backward

Bend at the waist forward and then backward to stretch the muscles in the upper body. Alternate between front and back, stretching four times in each direction.

During the first two stretches forward, place the hands on the floor and draw the hips back to stretch the spine. When performing the first two stretches backward, keep the hands on the hips.

During the last two stretches to the front, reach through the legs and concentrate on relaxing the spine. For the last two stretches to the back, reach back with the hands.

6) Body twisting

Twist the upper body around to the rear four times in the same direction, performing a different technique with each rotation—elbow strike, back-fist strike, ridge-hand strike, and lower-level spear hand. The same sequence is then repeated in the opposite direction.

When twisting to the left, use the left arm to first deliver an elbow strike, followed by a back-fist strike, then a ridge-

a. Elbow strike   b. Back-fist strike

hand strike, and finally a lower-level spear hand. The fourth and final rotation of each sequence should be held slightly longer than the preceding three rotations.

c. Ridge-hand strike   d. Spear hand

7) Body rotation

Rotate the upper body around in a full circle, first to the left, and then to the right. Alternate directions, stretching in each direction four times.

8) Legs stretches

a. Squat with one leg extended.
b. Bend at the waist over the extended leg.
c. Push the hips forward with the rear leg extended.

a   b   c

9) From square stance

a. Place the hands on the hip joints and press the hips down. This exercise provides stimulation to the hip joints.
b. Hold the ankles and use the elbows to press back against the knees. This exercise also targets the hip joints.
c. Place the hands on the knees and alternately push each shoulder down and to the front. This exercise stretches the spine.

a   b   c

10) Silent meditation

From a squatting position, propped up on the balls of the feet, gently close the eyes, push the crown of the head upward, and relax the arms in front of the body. Focus energy in the lower abdomen (roughly three fingers' width above the pubic bone). Difficulty in maintaining balance in the squatting position means that energy has not been sufficiently concentrated in the lower part of the abdomen.

11) From split-leg position

a. Spread the legs outward to each side and sit back on the floor. With practice, over time, almost anyone can perform this stretch.

b. With both legs extended to the sides, lean forward with the upper body and try to touch the chest and stomach to the floor while keeping the back extended. When performing this stretch, relax and imagine leading with the lower stomach. While stretching, it is important not to forget to breathe properly. Otherwise the muscles will resist the motion and become stiff.

c. With both legs extended to the sides, lean the upper body to one side. First, hold the ankle and press the side of the body against the leg. Next, extend the inside arm forward and twist the upper body slightly while pressing the side of the body against the leg. Each of these stretches should be performed four times to each side.

a   b

c

12) With legs extended forward

a. Grab the toes and pull them back to stretch the Achilles tendon. Hold this position for around 20 seconds.
b. Lean forward with the upper body while extending the arms in the direction of the feet. Try to relax fully while exhaling, drawing the chest down to the thighs without bending the knees.

a						b

13) With knees out and feet pulled inward

The following two streches, as well others in which the upper body leans forward, target the hips, which play a central role in karate movements. As such, these types of exercises need to be performed diligently and correctly.

a. With the heels drawn inward to the groin and the outer edges of the soles of the feet touching, press downward on the knees toward the floor. For people who are not able to touch their knees to the floor, another way to practice this exercise is to have someone stand on their legs just above the knees. To avoid possible injury, the person assisting must control the amount of weight he applies by holding on to the shoulders of the person performing the exercise.
b. Lean forward with the upper body while holding the feet. Pull the chest down toward the feet and use the elbows to press down on the legs.

a						b

14) With one leg extended forward and the other bent

The following exercises target primarily the spine and the hips. They should all be performed on both the left and right sides of the body.

a. This stretch is performed with one leg extended forward and the other bent, with the knee out to the side and the heel of the foot drawn toward the back of the hip. When the left leg is straight, as shown in the photo, hold the right ankle with the left hand and press against the inside of the left arm above the elbow with the right hand.

a

b

c

d

e

f

g

h

i

b. With the left hand positioned on the right ankle, reach back with the right hand while reclining the upper body.

c. Lean forward with the upper body in the direction of the extended leg.

d. Lean the upper body to the side in the direction of the leg that is bent.

e. Keeping the back straight, lean forward with the upper body, drawing the chest and stomach down toward the floor between the extended leg and the leg that is bent.

f. Without moving the location of the feet, raise the right knee so that the sole of the right foot rests flat on the floor. Press outward against the inside of the right knee with the right elbow.

g. Cross the right leg over the left, positioning the right foot on the far side of the left knee. Press outward against the right knee with the left elbow with the back straight and perpendicular to the floor.

h. With the left elbow against the right knee, extend the left arm outward in the direction of the left foot while reaching back with the right hand and reclining the upper body.

i. Cross the right leg over the left, resting the right ankle above the left knee. Hold the right leg in place above the ankle with the right hand and move the right foot around in a circular motion with the left hand to limber up the ankle joint.

15) Toe stretches

Sit in a kneeling position with the knees on the floor, the buttocks resting on the heels, and the backs of the feet facing the rear with the toes bent upward so that the bottoms of the toes press against the floor. Slide the knees forward and back several times to stretch the joints in the toes.

16) With feet turned out

Sit down between the heels of the feet with the buttocks touching the floor and the feet turned outward. People who are not able to touch the floor with their buttocks can use their hands to press down on their hips.

17) Knee exercises

a. Knee bends: With the feet closed, crouch down and hug the knees. From this position, stand up and fully extend the legs, pressing against the knees with the hands. Keep the heels against the floor throughout the exercise.

b. Knee rolls: With the knees slightly bent and the heels of the hands resting above the knees, guide the knees in a circular motion clockwise and then counterclockwise. This exercise is designed to prevent strain to the knees when kicking.

a   b

18) Limbering hands and feet

Shake out the hands and feet to loosen the joints in the wrists, fingers, ankles, and feet. As karate places demands on these joints, it is important for them to be well limbered.

19) Leg lifts

a. Standing in a front stance, sharply swing the rear leg forward and up in an arcing motion.

b. Standing with one foot just behind the other, sharply swing the rear leg out to the side and up in an arcing motion. When performing this exercise, compress the muscles at the flank (the side of the body between the ribs and hips).

c. Standing with the feet closed, sharply swing one leg back and up in an arc while looking over the shoulder on the same side as the leg being lifted. This exercise stretches the muscles in the back.

a   b   b

Sonoba-zuki (Punching while standing in place) その場突き

The basic training method for acquiring proper punching technique is *sonoba-zuki*, or punching while standing in place. Practicing *sonoba-zuki* requires a complete understanding of how the arms move in relation to each other when punching.

Sonoba-zuki: Overview of arm movements

1) Stand in an open V stance with both arms extended forward, the fists level with the solar plexus.
2) Pull the right fist back to above the hip with the back of the hand facing downward.
3) Move the right fist forward with the back of the hand facing downward until the elbow reaches the side of the body. At the same time, draw the left elbow straight back until it touches the side of the body, rotating the left fist 90 degrees so that the back of the hand faces outward.
4) Just prior to the moment of impact, rotate the right fist 90 degrees so that the back of the hand faces outward. At the same time, as the left fist nears the side of the body, rotate it 90 degrees so that the back of the hand faces downward.
5) At the moment of impact, immediately rotate the right fist so that the back of the hand faces upward while simultaneously pulling the left fist back to above the hip.

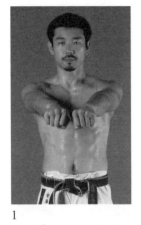

1

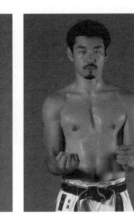

2

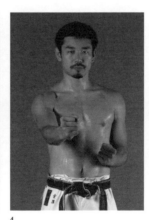

3

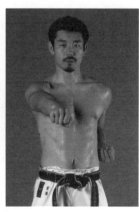

4

5

Once you have gained an understanding of the way in which the arms move when punching, it is time to begin practicing *sonoba-zuki*. At first, it is best to avoid trying to punch at full speed because the movement of the arms may not be properly synchronized. Initially, practice *sonoba-zuki* in stages, as described above.

Practicing sonoba-zuki

Stance: *Soto hachiji-dachi* (open V stance)

1) Stand in an open V stance with the left arm extended forward, the left hand positioned out in front of the body to protect the solar plexus and the right fist drawn back to above the hip.
2) Deliver a right middle-level straight punch.
3) Deliver a left middle-level straight punch.
   • Continue punching, alternating from left to right (around 50 punches).

1   2   3

Points to remember

1) As each arm travels either forward or back, the inside of the forearm and elbow should brush against the side of the body.
2) At the moment of impact, it is necessary to tighten the muscles along the side of the body below the armpit of the punching arm. If these muscles are not properly tensed, there is a tendency for the shoulder to rise.
3) Keep the back straight and extended with the feeling of pushing the crown of the head upward.
4) When delivering the punch, the fist should travel a straight path toward the target.

Mae-geri (Front snap kick) 1 前蹴り (一)

Mae-geri can be used to strike targets at various levels, including the stomach, chest and face. Although the ball of the foot (*koshi*) is commonly used as the striking surface when delivering a front snap kick, the instep (*haisoku*) and tips of the toes (*sokusō*) can also be used.

Practicing mae-geri 1

Stance: *Heisoku-dachi* (closed parallel stance)

1) Stand in a closed parallel stance with the knees slightly bent and the arms extended downward at an angle to the sides, as if holding a bucket of water in each hand.
2) Lift the right knee, drawing the foot alongside the left knee. The sole of the kicking foot should be kept parallel to the floor with the toes curled upward.
3) Deliver the kick with the feeling of striking the target with the knee of the kicking leg, using the snapping motion of the knee to generate speed and power. It is important to bend the ankle as the kicking leg reaches full extension, thrusting the ball of the foot toward the target. Upon kicking, immediately snap the leg back to the same position as shown in step 2.

1

2

3

4   5   6

4) Place the kicking foot on the floor and assume the original ready position.

5) Lift the left knee, following the same procedure as outlined in step 2.

6) Deliver the kick with the left leg in the same manner as described in step 3 and immediately snap the kicking leg back to the position shown in step 5. Then return the kicking foot to the floor and assume the ready position once again.

At first, *mae-geri* should be practiced in stages, as described above. Once you have gained an understanding of how the leg moves, the kick can be practiced from start to finish as a single continuous motion. Also, be aware of your breathing when you perform the kick. It should be in harmony with the movement: breathe out during the extension and withdrawal of the foot, and breathe in as the kicking foot returns to the floor.

Points to remember

1) The knee of the supporting leg should be kept slightly bent throughout.
2) Thrust the hips forward when delivering the kick.
3) The kicking leg should be fully extended at the moment of impact.
4) When standing on the supporting leg with the knee bent before and after kicking, focus energy in the lower abdomen to maintain balance.

Training method for beginner students

For beginning students, the level of effort required to maintain balance on one leg makes it difficult to concentrate on such points as using a snapping motion of the knee or fully extending the kicking leg at the moment of impact. The following exercise is designed to provide an easy means of acquiring the proper feel when performing a front snap kick.

1) Begin from a reclining position on the floor with the upper body propped up on the elbows and the hands beneath the lower back above the hips. Raise the right knee, drawing the heel of the foot toward the back of the hip while bending the ankle upward, pulling the instep toward the shin.
2) Kick upward toward the ceiling, keeping the ankle bent as the foot approaches the target.
3) At the moment of impact, fully extend the leg and thrust the ball of the foot out toward the target.
   • After completing the kick, retract the leg and return to the starting position.

The initial goal of this training method is to acquire the feel of fully extending the leg while thrusting the ball of the foot toward the target at the moment of impact. Next, this exercise should be practiced as a single flowing motion, focusing on the snapping motion of the knee to generate speed and power.

1

2

3

LESSON 2

- Lesson 1: Review (Approx. 30 min.)
- Zenkutsu-dachi (Front stance)
- Gyaku-zuki (Reverse punch)
- Mae-geri (Front snap kick) 2

Zenkutsu-dachi (Front stance) 前屈立ち

Shifting from an open V stance into a front stance is an important transition with applications for the practice of *kihon* (basics), *kumite* (sparring) and *kata* (form). Accordingly, it is essential to master moving correctly from one stance into the next.

Practicing zenkutsu-dachi

Stance: *Soto hachiji-dachi* (open V stance) to *zenkutsu-dachi* (front stance)

1) Stand in an open V stance with both arms extended downward in front of the body and the fists roughly shoulder-width apart.

2) Raise both arms, crossing the forearms in front of the chest to form a large X.

3) Step forward with the left leg into a left front stance. When stepping forward, the left foot describes an arc, as shown in the accompanying diagram, initially moving inward toward the opposite foot as it travels forward. At the same time, sharply pull the arms from their crossed position down and out to each side of the body with the feeling of ripping a cloth in two. The arms extend outward to the sides as if holding a bucket of water in each hand.

• Return to the initial open V stance by performing the movements described in steps 2 and 3 in reverse.

• Following the same procedure, also practice shifting into a right front stance by stepping forward with the right leg.

1

2

Points to remember

1) When practicing *zenkutsu-dachi*, there is a tendency to move the stepping foot in a straight line. Make sure that the foot describes a curved path as it moves into place.

2) To prevent the upper body from leaning forward at the instant the step is complete, lead into the step with the hips, keeping the back straight and extended.

3

Gyaku-zuki (Reverse punch) 逆突き

Gyaku-zuki, in which the punch is performed using the arm on the side opposite to the front leg, is one of the fundamental punches used in karate.

Practicing chūdan (middle-level) gyaku-zuki

Stance: *Zenkutsu-dachi* (front stance)

1) Stand in a left front stance with the hips at *hanmi* (45-degree angle to the front). The left arm is extended forward with the hand positioned out in front of the body to protect the solar plexus and the right fist is drawn back to above the hip.

2) Keeping the hips at *hanmi*, move the right fist forward with the back of the hand facing downward until the elbow reaches the side of the body. At the same time, draw the left elbow back halfway, rotating the left hand 90 degrees so that the back of the hand faces outward.

3) Turn the hips toward the front while delivering the reverse punch, rotating the right fist so that the back of the hand faces upward. Pull the left hand back to above the hip while forming it into a fist, rotating it 90 degrees so that the back of the hand faces downward.

   • Upon completing the punch, immediately return to the original ready position.

At first, *chūdan gyaku-zuki* should be practiced in stages, as described above. Then, practice the technique as a single continuous motion.

Points to remember

1) Turn the hips sharply between steps 2 and 3.
2) Both the punching and pulling arms should brush against the side of the body as they travel along their respective courses.

1   2   3

Mae-geri (Front snap kick) 2 前蹴り (二)

Practicing mae-geri 2

Stance: *Zenkutsu-dachi* (front stance)

1) Stand in a left front stance with the hips facing the front and the fists out to the sides.

2) Lift the right knee with the feeling of striking the target with the knee, drawing the right foot alongside the left knee. The sole of the kicking foot should be kept parallel to the floor with the toes curled upward. Keep the knee of the supporting leg bent at the same angle as it was in step 1.

3) Deliver an upper-level front snap kick using the snapping motion of the knee. The kicking leg, rebounding from the kick, immediately returns to the same position as shown in step 2.

 • After kicking, return to the original ready position.

At first, practice *mae-geri* 2 in stages, as described above, then as a single continuous motion.

Points to remember

1) When lifting the knee prior to kicking and when returning to *zenkutsu-dachi* following the kick, the kicking foot should travel in a straight line.

2) When the kicking leg is raised, there is a tendency to lean the upper body forward or back to maintain balance. Focusing energy in the lower abdomen will enable improved balance.

3) When lifting the knee prior to kicking, keep the knee of the supporting leg bent.

4) When delivering the kick, thrust the hips forward toward the target.

1

2

3

- Lesson 2: Review (Approx. 30 min.)
- Oi-zuki (Lunge punch) 1
- Gedan-barai (Downward block)
- Oi-zuki 2
- Mae-geri (Front snap kick) 3
- Tenshin (Body rotation) with gedan-barai

Oi-zuki (Lunge punch) 1 追い突き（一）

Like *gyaku-zuki* (reverse punch), *oi-zuki* is one of the fundamental punches used in karate. In *oi-zuki*, the punch is performed using the arm on the same side as the leg positioned in front. This type of punch is also called *jun-zuki* (front punch).

Practicing chūdan (middle-level) oi-zuki 1

Stance: *Soto hachiji-dachi* (open V stance) to *zenkutsu-dachi* (front stance)

1) Stand in an open V stance with the left arm extended forward, the left hand positioned out in front of the body to protect the solar plexus, and the right fist drawn back to above the hip.
2) Maintaining the same upper-body posture, draw the right foot in toward the left foot while bending the knees and lowering the hips.
3) Push the left hand forward while advancing the right foot one half-step.
4) Advance the right foot the remaining half-step into a front stance while simultaneously delivering a middle-level punch with the right fist. At the same time, pull the left hand back to above the hip while forming it into a fist.
   • After delivering the punch, return to the original ready position.

At first, practice in stages, as described above, then as a single continuous motion.

Points to remember

1) Pushing the left hand forward in step 3 serves to drive the left hip forward so that the hips are nearly at *gyaku-hanmi* (45-degree angle to the front, with the hip on the side opposite to the front leg pushed forward). This enables the hips to be turned toward the front when performing the technique, which increases the destructive force of the punch.
2) Do not use the arm alone when punching. Thrust off the heel of the rear foot and extend the rear leg when delivering the punch for a more powerful and more effective technique.
3) Make sure that the stepping foot describes a curved path as it moves from *soto hachiji-dachi* into *zenkutsu-dachi*.

1

2

3

4

Gedan-barai (Downward block) 下段払い

In *gedan-barai*, a sweeping block that travels downward at an angle, the outside of the wrist is used to deflect punches or kicks aimed at the lower abdomen.

Gedan-barai: Overview of arm movements

1) Stand in an open V stance with the left fist positioned above the right shoulder and the back of the hand facing outward. The right arm is extended to the front and downward at an angle to protect the front of the body.

2) Draw the left arm downward from the elbow at an angle without rotating the left fist. At the same time, pull the right elbow back toward the body.

3) Continue to drive the left fist downward at an angle but do not rotate it until just before the block has been completed. Rotate the right fist as it approaches the side of the body so that the back of the hand faces outward.

4) Follow through with the left arm to complete the block, rotating the left fist so that the back of the hand faces upward. At the same time, firmly pull the right fist back to above the hip with the back of the hand facing downward.

   • Upon completing the block, continue to practice using the opposite side, returning to step 1 by drawing the right fist up to the left shoulder and extending the left arm in front of the body and downward at an angle.

Points to remember

1) The blocking hand describes a curved path centered on the shoulder and elbow.

2) Waiting until just before completing the block to rotate the fist of the blocking arm enables a more powerful and effective technique.

3) In the completed position, the blocking arm extends downward at a 45-degree angle. The distance between the elbow of the blocking arm and the body should be roughly equivalent to the width of your fist.

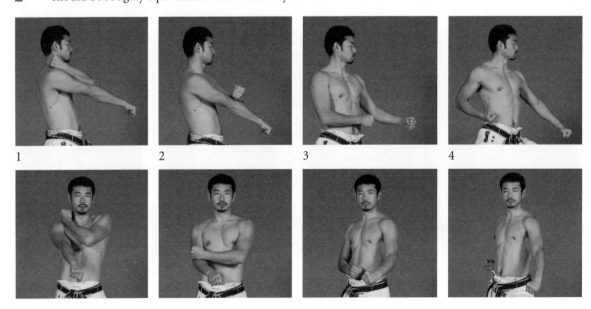

1   2   3   4

Practicing gedan-barai

Once you have gained an understanding of how the arms move in *gedan-barai*, it is time to begin practicing the technique while stepping forward into a front stance

Stance: *Soto hachiji-dachi* (open V stance) to *zenkutsu-dachi* (front stance)

1) Stand in an open V stance with both arms extended downward in front of the body and the fists roughly shoulder-width apart.
2) Draw the left fist back to above the right shoulder with the back of the hand facing outward and extend the right arm to the front and downward. At the same time, pull the left foot in toward the right foot while bending the knees deeply.
3) Push the right hand forward while advancing the left foot one half-step.
4) Advance the left foot the remaining half-step into a front stance while simultaneously performing a downward block. When delivering the block, use a large sweeping motion with the fist while turning the hips to *hanmi* (45-degree angle to the front).
   • Return to step 1 and repeat several times.

FRONT ————————————————————————————————→

1   2   3   4

Practicing gedan-barai while stepping back

Stance: *Soto hachiji-dachi* (open V stance) to *zenkutsu-dachi* (front stance)

1) Stand in an open V stance with both arms extended downward in front of the body and the fists roughly shoulder-width apart.
2) Pull the right foot in toward the left foot while bending the knees deeply. At the same time, draw the left fist back to above the right shoulder with the back of the hand facing outward, and extend the right arm to the front and downward.
3) Push the right hand forward while taking one half-step back with the right foot.
4) Take the remaining half-step back with the right foot into a front stance while simultaneously performing a downward block.
   • Return to step 1 and repeat several times.

Points to remember

1) At the instant that the block is delivered, sharply extend the rear leg with the feeling of thrusting off the floor with the rear foot.
2) Do not lean forward or back when performing *gedan-barai*; keep the upper body perpendicular to the floor throughout the exercise.
3) Turn the hips sharply while delivering the block, beginning with the hips facing the front throughout the first half-step, and finishing with the hips at *hanmi*.

BACK

Oi-zuki (Lunge punch) 2 追い突き (二)

This exercise is the first to employ a complete stepping technique. The use of the legs when advancing or retreating in karate, called *unsoku*, differs greatly from the steps we take when walking. As such, beginning students should practice this exercise until they become comfortable with the movements.

Practicing chūdan (middle-level) oi-zuki 2

Stance: *Zenkutsu-dachi* (front stance) to *zenkutsu-dachi*

1) Assume a left downward-block ready position standing in a left front stance with the hips at *hanmi* (45-degree angle to the front).

2) Draw the right leg forward, positioning the right foot alongside the left foot. Keep the left knee bent at the same angle and bend the right knee as it advances. The upper body remains in the same posture.

3) Keeping the left arm extended downward at an angle, push the left fist forward while advancing the right foot one half-step. The right fist remains positioned above the hip.

4) Advance the right foot the remaining half-step into a right front stance while simultaneously performing a right middle-level lunge punch.

1   2

3   4

5   6   7

5) Step forward with the left leg, placing the left foot beside the right foot. The right knee remains bent at the same angle and the left knee bends as it advances. The upper body does not move.

6) Push the right fist forward while advancing the left foot one half-step. The left fist remains pulled back to above the hip.

7) Advance the left foot the remaining half-step into a left front stance while delivering a left middle-level lunge punch.

   • Proceed to step 2 and continue stepping forward while delivering middle-level lunge punches.

At first, practice each step forward in stages, as described above, then as a single continuous motion, advancing several steps at a time.

Points to remember

1) When drawing the rear leg alongside the front leg, the knees tend to straighten, which raises the height of the hips. Pay special attention to ensure that both knees are bent so that the hips remain at the same height throughout the technique.

2) When executing the punch, sharply extend the rear leg with the feeling of thrusting off the floor with the rear foot. The reaction will enable the delivery of a more powerful and more effective punch.

3) Keep the back straight and extended throughout the exercise.

Mae-geri (Front snap kick) **3** 前蹴り（三）

Practicing mae-geri 3

Stance: *Zenkutsu-dachi* (front stance) to *zenkutsu-dachi*

1) Stand in a left front stance with the hips facing the front and the fists down and out to the sides.

2) Lift the right knee so that the right foot describes a straight line as it travels to its position beside the left knee. Keep the knee of the supporting leg bent at the same angle as it was in step 1.

3) Deliver a right front snap kick using the snapping motion of the knee. Thrust the hips forward when delivering the kick for a more powerful attack.

   • Return the right foot back to beside the left knee while straightening the left leg toward the front, advancing the center of gravity forward. As the left leg becomes fully extended, step forward with the right leg into a right front stance. The right foot describes a straight line as it moves from its position beside the left knee to the floor.

   • Next, following the steps outlined above for the opposite side, deliver a front snap kick with the left leg. Proceed forward in the same manner for several more steps.

Points to remember

1) When lifting the knee prior to kicking and after retracting the leg following the kick, bend the knee of the supporting leg.

2) When kicking, do not lean back with the upper body.

1

2

3

Tenshin (Body rotation) with gedan-barai 下段払いによる転身

When performing techniques while stepping forward, it will become necessary at some point to turn around to continue practicing. This exercise provides a means of reversing directions using *tenshin*, or body rotation, while performing a downward block.

Practicing tenshin using gedan-barai

Stance: *Zenkutsu-dachi* (front stance) to *zenkutsu-dachi*

1) Assume a right downward-block ready position standing in a right front stance with the hips at *hanmi* (45-degree angle to the front).
2) Pivoting on the front foot, shift the rear leg to the right while drawing the left fist to above the right shoulder. At the same time, extend the right arm out in front of the left side of the chest.
3) Shift into a left front stance facing the opposite direction while performing a left downward block.

Points to remember

The original meaning of *tenshin* refers to the ability to freely turn the body so as to face any direction. When mastered, *tenshin*, a highly advanced technical skill, enables karate practitioners to immediately block an attack, regardless of the direction from which it may come, and respond with a counterattack. As such, the eventual goal should be the ability to apply *tenshin* in any direction and with any technique.

1

2

3

空手

CHAPTER 2

Expanding on the Basics

LESSON 4

- ■ Lessons 1–3: Review (Approx. 40 min.)
- ■ Uraken-uchi (Back-fist strike)
- ■ Kiba-dachi (Straddle-leg stance)
- ■ Empi-uchi (Elbow strike)
- ■ Yoko-geri ke-age (Side snap kick)

Uraken-uchi (Back-fist strike) 裏拳打ち

Uraken-uchi can be used for attacks targeting the face and solar plexus. To ensure an effective back-fist strike, use the arm like a whip, with a snapping motion of the elbow and wrist.

Uraken-uchi: Overview of arm movements

There are two types of back-fist strike, depending on the path that the arm travels: side round back-fist strike and vertical round back-fist strike.

Yoko-mawashi uraken-uchi (Side round back-fist strike)

1) Begin with the right fist pressed against the right nipple and the back of the hand facing upward. The right forearm is parallel to the floor with the elbow pointing out to the side and the left fist is drawn back to above the hip.

2) Launch the right fist on an arcing path centered on the elbow so that the forearm travels on a plane parallel to the floor. The back of the hand remains facing upward as the fist approaches its target.

3) At the moment of impact, expand the chest and rotate the wrist 90 degrees so that the thumb side of the fist faces upward. The left fist remains pulled back, positioned above the hip.

1   2   3

Tate-mawashi uraken-uchi (Vertical round back-fist strike)

1) As with *yoko-mawashi uraken-uchi*, begin with the right fist pressed against the right nipple and the back of the hand facing upward. The right elbow points out to the side and the left fist is pulled back to above the hip.

2) Launch the right fist on a vertical arcing path centered on the elbow so that the fist travels in front of the face with the back of the hand facing in the direction of the target.

3) The fist travels downward toward the target with the back of the hand also facing downward. The left fist remains positioned above the hip.

1

2

3

Points to remember

1) The effectiveness of a back-fist strike depends on the snapping motion of the elbow and wrist at the moment of impact.

2) When performing a back-fist strike, the forearm should move in a large and dynamic sweeping motion.

3) Expand the chest fully at the moment of impact to generate a more powerful and more effective technique.

Practicing uraken-uchi 1

Stance: *Soto hachiji-dachi* (Open V stance)

Stand in an open V stance and, following the steps outlined in the preceding "Overview of arm movements" section, practice performing back-fist strikes slowly. Once you become comfortable with the motion, gradually increase speed.

Practicing uraken-uchi 2

Stance: *Soto hachiji-dachi* (open V stance)

1) Stand in an open V stance with both fists in front of the chest and the backs of the hands facing upward. The elbows point out to each side and the face is turned to the right, in the direction of the initial target.
2) Deliver a side round back-fist strike with the right fist.
3) Immediately pull back the fist to its original ready position and turn the head to face the left.
4) Deliver a side round back-fist strike to the left.
5) Immediately return the left fist to its original ready position and turn the head to face the right.

1   2   3   4

5   6   7   8

6) Deliver a vertical round back-fist strike with the right fist.

7) Immediately pull back the fist and turn the head to face the left.

8) Deliver a vertical round back-fist strike with the left fist.

- Immediately pull back the striking fist and repeat the entire sequence from step 1, practicing the sequence several times in succession.

Points to remember

1) In *yoko-mawashi uraken-uchi*, the fist travels along an arc that is parallel to the floor; in *tate-mawashi uraken-uchi*, it travels along an arc that is perpendicular to the floor. When practicing back-fist strikes, it should be clear which type you are performing from the path the fist travels.

2) Make use of the snapping motion of the elbow and wrist for a more effective technique.

3) At the moment of impact, expand the chest fully to generate additional power.

Kiba-dachi (Straddle-leg stance) 騎馬立ち

Shifting from an open V stance into a straddle-leg stance is important not only for learning transitions between differing stances, but also for practicing how to tense certain muscles in the legs.

Practicing kiba-dachi

Stance: *Soto hachiji-dachi* (open V stance) to *kiba-dachi* (straddle-leg stance)

1

1) Stand in an open V stance with both arms extended downward in front of the body and the fists roughly shoulder-width apart.

When shifting into a straddle-leg stance from an open V stance, raise both arms, crossing the forearms in front of the chest to form a large X.

2) Step forward into the straddle-leg stance so that the body faces the side, extending both arms downward in a large motion to the sides. The head remains facing the front throughout. Make sure that the straddle-leg stance is being performed properly, keeping the muscles in the legs tensed for about ten seconds.

- Return to the original ready position and repeat the exercise several times.

2

Empi-uchi (Elbow strike) 猿臂打ち（肘当て）

In *empi-uchi*, also called *hiji-ate*, the elbow is used to strike the target. Elbow strikes are effective techniques at close range and are well suited for self-defense applications.

Empi-uchi: Overview of arm movements

Depending on the movement of the arm, seven different elbow strikes are possible.

1. Mae empi-uchi (Forward elbow strike)

When delivering a forward elbow strike, the fist of the striking arm travels across the chest to the nipple on the opposite side as the arm moves along the side of the body. Drive the elbow forward for strikes targeting the chest, solar plexus and side of the body.

2. Yoko empi-uchi (Side elbow strike)

1) Fully extend the right arm to the left side and up at an angle so that the hand is slightly higher than the shoulder. The hand is open with the palm facing upward.

2) Thrust the right elbow out to the right side while drawing the forearm across the chest. At the same time, form the right hand into a fist and rotate it so that the back of the hand faces outward. Do not allow the fist to rotate any further until just before the moment of impact.

3) Complete the strike, thrusting the right elbow to the side until the fist is in front of the right nipple. At the moment of impact, rotate the fist so that the back of the hand faces upward.

Side elbow strikes can be used for attacks to the chest, solar plexus and side of the body.

1   2   3

3. Ushiro empi-uchi (Back elbow strike)

When performing *ushiro empi-uchi*, the striking arm is first extended toward the front. Drive the elbow straight back with the back of the fist facing downward, drawing the forearm along the side of the body. Back elbow strikes can be used for attacks to the rear, targeting the chest and solar plexus.

4. Mae mawashi empi-uchi (Forward round elbow strike)

1) Begin with the left arm extended forward, the left hand positioned out in front of the body, and the right fist drawn back to above the hip.
2) Moving the arms in the same manner as the first step when performing a punch, pull the left elbow back while moving the right arm forward along the side of the body.
3) Continue pulling the left elbow back while moving the right fist along the chest toward the left nipple. The right elbow begins to describe an arc around the side of the body.
4) As the right fist reaches the left nipple, drive the right elbow forward. At the same time, pull the left fist back to above the hip.

Forward round elbow strikes can be used for attacks targeting the side of the body.

1   2   3   4

5. Ushiro-mawashi empi-uchi (Back round elbow strike)

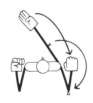

To perform *ushiro-mawashi empi-uchi*, begin with the striking arm extended forward at an angle so that, when viewed from the front, the hand is aligned with the opposite side of the body. The hand is open and raised slightly higher than the shoulder with the palm facing upward. Drive the elbow out to the side and back in an arcing motion while forming the hand into a fist, rotating it so that the back of the hand faces upward. The opposite hand remains pulled back, positioned above the hip.

Back round elbow strikes are effective in attacks directed to the face, chest, and side of the body.

6. Tate empi-uchi (Upward elbow strike)

1) Begin with the left arm extended forward, the left hand positioned out in front of the body and the right fist drawn back to above the hip.

2) Pull the left elbow back halfway to the point where it comes in contact with the side of the body. Draw the right arm forward by rotating the shoulder, keeping the elbow bent at the same angle and the fist positioned so that the thumb side of the hand continues facing outward.

3) Continue the arm movements initiated in step 2, pulling the left elbow back further and raising the right elbow upward.

4) Complete the strike with a large upward swing of the right elbow, drawing the right fist down alongside the right ear while rotating the fist so that the back of the hand faces outward. At the same time, pull the left fist back to above the hip.

Upward elbow strikes can be used for attacks to the chin.

1

2

3

4

7. Otoshi empi-uchi (Downward elbow strike)

Beginning with the striking arm extended toward the ceiling, drop the elbow straight down, bending it so that at the moment of impact the forearm is perpendicular to the floor with the back of the fist facing the front.

Downward elbow strikes can be directed to the face and solar plexus in situations where these targets are positioned at a relatively low level.

Practicing yoko empi-uchi

Stance: *Soto hachiji-dachi* (open V stance) to *kiba-dachi* (straddle-leg stance)

1) Stand in an open V stance with the right arm extended to the left side and up at an angle so that the hand is slightly higher than the shoulder. The hand is open with the palm up and the face is turned to the right, in the direction of the target.

1

2) Deliver a right side elbow strike while stepping with the right foot to the side, shifting into a straddle-leg stance. At the moment of impact expand the chest fully to ensure an effective technique.

   • Return to the original ready position by drawing the right foot inward and repeat the exercise several times.

Points to remember

Time the rotation of the fist so that it coincides with the moment of impact.

2

Practicing mae mawashi empi-uchi

Stance: *Zenkutsu-dachi* (front stance)

1) Stand in a left front stance with the hips at *hanmi* (45-degree angle to the front). The left arm is extended forward with the hand positioned out in front of the body to protect the solar plexus and the right fist is drawn back to above the hip.

1

2) Drive the right elbow forward in a large sweeping motion around the side of the body while turning the hips to the front. To support the turning motion of the hips, pull the left hand back strongly to above the hip.

   • Return to the original ready position and repeat the exercise several times.

Points to remember

Do not try to strike with the motion of the arm alone. It is important to make full use of the turning of the hips and the pulling hand to deliver a powerful and effective technique.

2

Practicing tate empi-uchi

Stance: *Zenkutsu-dachi* (front stance)

1) Stand in a left front stance with the hips at *hanmi* (45-degree angle to the front). The left arm is extended forward with the hand positioned out in front of the body to protect the solar plexus and the right fist is drawn back to above the hip.
2) Swing the right elbow up while turning the hips to the front. Pull the left hand back sharply and fully expand the chest vertically.
   • Return to the original ready position and repeat the exercise several times.

Points to remember

1) It is important to use the rotation of the hips effectively to deliver a powerful strike.
2) Do not lean back when performing *tate empi-uchi*; keep the upper body perpendicular to the floor throughout the exercise.

1   2

Practicing empi-uchi combinations

Stance: *Zenkutsu-dachi* (front stance) to *kiba-dachi* (straddle-leg stance) to *zenkutsu-dachi*

1) Stand in a left front stance with the hips at *hanmi* (45-degree angle to the front). The left arm is extended forward with the hand positioned out in front of the body to protect the solar plexus and the right fist is drawn back to above the hip.
2) Deliver a forward round elbow strike, driving the right elbow forward in a large sweeping motion around the side of the body while turning the hips to the front. At the same time, pull the left hand back to above the hip.
3) Deliver an upward elbow strike, swinging the left elbow up while turning the hips 45 degrees to *hanmi*. At the same time, pull the right hand back to above the hip.
4) Shifting the body's weight to the right leg, extend the left arm to the right side and up at an angle so that the hand is slightly higher than the shoulder with the palm facing upward. The left hand passes over the head and opens as it travels to the opposite side of the body.

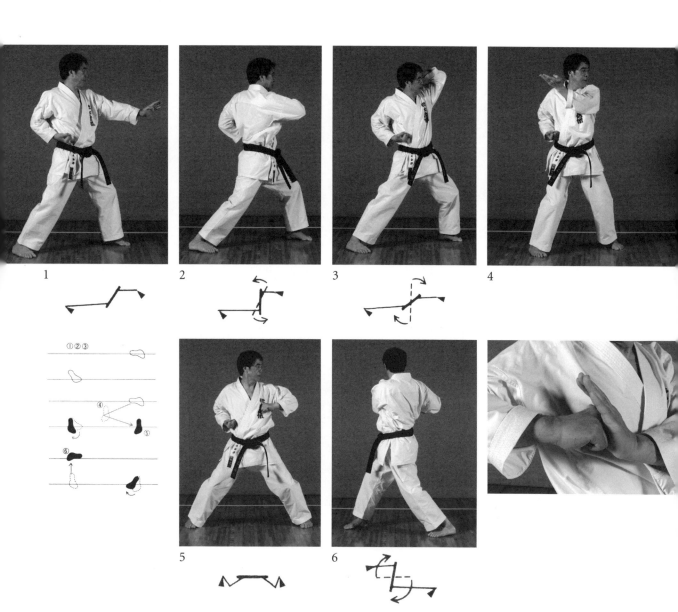

1

2

3

4

5

6

5) Deliver a side elbow strike to the left, thrusting off the right foot and shifting into a straddle-leg stance so that the body faces the side.

6) Deliver a back round elbow strike with the right arm, drawing the right foot back into a front stance facing the rear while swinging the elbow around in a large sweeping motion.

• Perform a left downward block to the front and return to the original ready position.

Points to remember

1) Each of the four elbow strikes in this exercise utilizes the hips in a different way. It is important to use the hips correctly and effectively for each technique.

2) To increase the effectiveness of the final *ushiro-mawashi empi-uchi*, use the opposite hand to push against the fist as the elbow approaches the target.

Yoko-geri ke-age (Side snap kick) 横蹴上げ

In *yoko-geri ke-age*, also called *yoko ke-age*, the outer edge of the foot (*sokutō*) is used to strike middle-level or upper-level targets, including the face, jaw or side of the body.

Practicing yoko-geri ke-age 1

Stance: *Heisoku-dachi* (closed parallel stance)

1) Stand in a closed parallel stance with the fists out to the sides, and the knees bent slightly.
2) Turn the head to face the left side and lift the left knee, positioning the outer edge of the foot against the inside of the supporting leg above the knee. Apply outward pressure to the left knee, pointing it in the direction of the target.
3) Deliver a left side snap kick, swinging the leg up sharply in a large arcing motion and using the snapping motion of the knee to generate speed and power at the moment of impact. When kicking, draw the left hand back behind the kicking leg.
   • Upon delivering the kick, immediately snap the leg back to the same position as step 2.
   • Return to the original ready position and repeat the exercise several times.

Points to remember

1) Keep the supporting leg bent slightly throughout the technique.
2) Deliver the kick with the feeling of striking the target with the knee and the hip of the kicking leg. At the same time, compress the muscles at the flank (the side of the body between the ribs and hips).
3) Do not allow the upper body to lean too far forward when kicking.

1   2   3

Training method for beginning students

For beginning students, performing kicks to the front is relatively easy compared with kicking to the side. The following exercise provides an easy means of getting used to the feeling of kicking to the side.

1) Begin from a reclining position with the left side of the body against the floor, the upper body propped up on the left elbow. Rest the outer edge of the right foot against the inside of the left thigh with the right knee pointing upright.
2) Raise the right foot upward so that the path of the foot describes an arc centered on the knee.
3) Once the right leg reaches full extension, hold it near the ankle with the right hand and make sure that the foot is positioned properly, with the outer edge of the foot facing upward.
   • Return to the original ready position and repeat the exercise several times.

At first, practice the exercise in stages, as described above. Once you become more comfortable with the movement, practice the exercise as a single continuous motion, using the snapping motion of the knee at the moment of impact.

1

2

3

Practicing yoko-geri ke-age 2

Stance: *Kiba-dachi* (straddle-leg stance) to *kiba-dachi*

1) Stand in a straddle-leg stance with the fists out to the sides and the head turned facing the right.
2) Keeping the knees bent, draw the left leg in and place the left foot on the far side of the right foot. Do not allow the hips to rise or the posture of the upper body to change.
3) Lift the right knee, drawing the foot up behind the left leg until the instep rests against the back of the left knee. The right knee points in the direction of the target.
4) Deliver a right side snap kick with the feeling of striking the target with the knee and the hip of the kicking leg, using the snapping motion of the knee to generate speed and power.
5) Immediately snap the kicking leg back, retracting the right foot to above the left knee.
6) Step forward with the right leg into a straddle-leg stance.
   • Proceed to step 2 and continue practicing the exercise.

Points to remember

1) When crossing the legs in step 2, keep the legs bent sufficiently to ensure that the hips do not rise. The hips should remain at the same height throughout the exercise.
2) There is a tendency not to raise the knee fully prior to executing the kick. Lifting the knee high in the direction of the target enables the delivery of a swift and powerful kick.

1

2

3

4

5

6

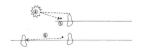

LESSON 5

Jōdan age-uke (Upper-level rising block) 上段揚受け

In *jōdan age-uke*, one of the fundamental blocks employed in karate, the forearm of the blocking arm is thrust upward and the outside of the wrist is used to deflect punches aimed at the face.

Jōdan age-uke: Overview of arm movements

1) Stand in an open V stance with the right arm extended upward at an angle in front of the body and the right hand formed into a knife hand (*shutō*). The left fist is pulled back to above the hip.

2) Pull the right elbow downward while raising the left arm so that the wrists cross in front of the chest. The blocking arm (left arm) passes on the outside of the pulling arm.

3) Raise the left forearm to complete the block, rotating the fist so that the little-finger side of the hand faces upward. At the same time, pull the right hand back to above the hip while forming it into a fist. The blocking arm is bent at an angle greater than 90 degrees and the distance between the forehead and the blocking arm should be roughly equivalent to the width of your fist.

1   2   3

Practicing jōdan age-uke 1

Stance: *Soto hachiji-dachi* (open V stance) to *zenkutsu-dachi* (front stance)

1) Stand in an open V stance with both arms extended downward in front of the body and the fists roughly shoulder-width apart.

2) Pull the left foot in toward the right foot while thrusting the right hand upward at an angle in front of the body. At the same time, pull the left hand back to above the hip while forming it into a fist. Bend both knees and keep the hips facing the front.

3) With the feeling of pushing the right hand forward and pulling the left fist back, advance the left foot one half-step, keeping the hips facing the front.

4) Advance the left foot the remaining half-step into a front stance while simultaneously performing an upper-level rising block with the left arm. When delivering the block, turn the hips 45 degrees to *hanmi*.

• Return to step 1 and repeat several times.

1

2

3

4

Points to remember

1) Pushing the right hand forward and pulling the left hand back while stepping forward (step 3) serves to ensure that the hips face the front through the first half-step. This will enable a greater range of motion when turning the hips, making possible a stronger and more effective *age-uke*. The feeling should be of blocking with the hips.

2) Expand the chest fully when blocking but keep the upper body straight and perpendicular to the floor throughout the technique.

Practicing jōdan age-uke 2

Stepping forward

Stance: *Zenkutsu-dachi* (front stance) to *zenkutsu-dachi*

1) Assume a left downward-block ready position standing in a left front stance with the hips at *hanmi* (45-degree angle to the front).

2) Keeping the left knee bent at the same angle, bring the right foot forward to beside the left foot while thrusting the left hand upward at an angle in front of the body. The right fist remains above the hip and the hips face the front.

3) With the feeling of pushing the left hand forward and pulling the right fist back, advance the right foot one half-step, keeping the hips facing the front.

4) Advance the right foot the remaining half-step into a front stance, delivering the rising block while turning the hips 45 degrees to *hanmi*.

- Following the steps outlined above for the opposite side, step forward with the left leg while delivering an upper-level rising block with the left arm. Proceed forward in the same manner for several steps.

Stepping back

5) (From a right front stance) Keeping the right knee bent at the same angle, draw the right foot back to beside the left foot while thrusting the right hand upward at an angle in front of the body. The left fist remains above the hip and the hips face the front.

6) With the feeling of pushing the right hand forward and pulling the left fist back, draw the right foot back one half-step, keeping the hips facing the front.

7) Draw the right foot back the remaining half-step into a front stance, delivering a rising block with the left arm while turning the hips 45 degrees to *hanmi*.
   • Following the steps outlined above for the opposite side, step back with the left leg while delivering a rising block with the right arm. Continue stepping back in the same manner for several steps.

Points to remember

1) The hips remain at the same height throughout the exercise.
2) Keep the upper body straight and perpendicular to the floor throughout the technique.
3) Emphasizing the turning of the hips when delivering the block will lead to the development of a powerful blocking technique.

5   6   7

1

2

3

4

Chūdan soto ude-uke
(Middle-level outside-to-inside block) 中段外受け

In *soto ude-uke*, also called *soto-uke*, the fist of the blocking arm travels along a curved path from the side of the body to the front, with the little-finger side of the wrist used to deflect the attack. *Chūdan* (middle-level) *soto ude-uke* can be used to block punches and kicks targeting the chest area.

Chūdan soto ude-uke: Overview of arm movements

1) Stand in an open V stance with the left elbow pulled back to the side and bent so that the fist is positioned beside the left ear. The left wrist is turned outward so that the back of the hand faces the side of the head. The right arm is extended forward with the hand positioned out in front of the body to protect the solar plexus.

2) Draw the left arm around to the front by rotating the shoulder. The left fist describes a gradually descending arc but the wrist stays locked so that the fist does not rotate. At the same time, pull the right elbow back toward the body, rotating the right hand while forming it into a fist.

3) Continue to draw the blocking arm around to the front of the body but keep the wrist locked until just before the block has been completed.

4) Complete the block by rotating the fist a little beyond the point where the back of the hand faces the front. At the same time, pull the right fist back to above the hip.

• Following the steps outlined above for the opposite side, practice performing middle-level outside-to-inside blocks with the right arm.

Points to remember

1) Rotating the fist of the blocking arm at the moment contact is made enables even strong attacks to be blocked with relative ease.

2) Upon completing the block, the elbow of the blocking arm is bent at a 90-degree angle and the distance between the upper arm and the body should be roughly equivalent to the width of your fist. This should bring the fist of the blocking arm level with the shoulder.

Practicing chūdan soto ude-uke 1

Stance: *Soto hachiji-dachi* (open V stance) to *zenkutsu-dachi* (front stance)

1) Stand in an open V stance with both arms extended downward in front of the body and the fists roughly shoulder-width apart.

2) Pull the right foot in toward the left foot and bend the knees while pulling the right elbow to the side and back so that the fist is positioned beside the right ear. At the same time, extend the left arm out in front of the body.

3) With the feeling of pushing the left hand forward and pulling the right shoulder back, advance the right foot one half-step, keeping the hips facing the front.

4) Advance the right foot the remaining half-step into a front stance while simultaneously performing a middle-level outside-to-inside block. When delivering the block, turn the hips 45 degrees to *hanmi*.

• Return to step 1 and repeat several times.

Points to remember

1) Keeping the hips facing the front through step 3 will lead to the development of a powerful blocking technique.

2) Keep the upper body straight and perpendicular to the floor when blocking.

3) When blocking, tighten the muscles along the side of the body below the armpit of the blocking arm. If these muscles are not properly tensed, there is a tendency for the shoulder to rise.

1

2

3

4

Practicing chūdan soto ude-uke 2

Stepping forward

Stance: *Zenkutsu-dachi* (front stance) to *zenkutsu-dachi*

1) Assume a left downward-block ready position standing in a left front stance with the hips at *hanmi* (45-degree angle to the front).

2) Keeping the left knee bent at the same angle, draw the right foot forward to beside the left foot. At the same time, pull the right fist back to beside the right ear while extending the left arm out in front of the body.

3) Advance the right foot one half-step, keeping the hips facing the front.

4) Advance the right foot the remaining half-step into a front stance, simultaneously performing a middle-level outside-to-inside block while turning the hips 45 degrees to *hanmi*.

   • Following the steps outlined above for the opposite side, advance with the left leg while delivering a middle-level outside-to-inside block with the left arm. Proceed forward in the same manner for several steps.

Stepping back

5) (From a right front stance) Keeping the right knee bent at the same angle, draw the right foot back to beside the left foot. At the same time, pull the left fist back to beside the left ear while extending the right arm out in front of the body.

6) Draw the right foot back one half-step, keeping the hips facing the front.

7) Draw the right foot back the remaining half-step into a front stance, delivering an outside-to-inside block with the left arm while turning the hips 45 degrees to *hanmi*.

   • Following the steps outlined above for the opposite side, step back with the left leg while delivering an outside-to-inside block with the right arm. Continue stepping back in the same manner for several steps.

5

6

7

1

2

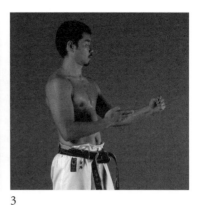

3

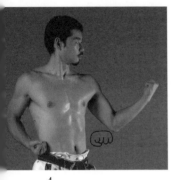

4

Uchi ude-uke (Inside-to-outside block) 内腕受け

In *uchi ude-uke*, also called *uchi-uke*, the fist of the blocking arm travels laterally in front of the chest and the thumb side of the wrist is used to deflect the attack. *Chūdan* (middle-level) *uchi ude-uke* can be used to block punches aimed at the chest area.

Chūdan uchi ude-uke: Overview of arm movements

1) Stand in an open V stance with the left fist positioned below the right underarm and the back of the hand facing upward. The right arm is extended forward with the hand open in front of the body.

2) Pull the right elbow back toward the body while drawing the left fist out, using the elbow as a pivot. The left fist travels along a path just outside the right elbow.

3) While pulling the right elbow back, continue to draw the blocking arm out, rotating the forearm of the blocking arm so that the thumb side of the fist faces upward.

4) Complete the block by drawing the forearm out, rotating the fist a little beyond the point where the back of the hand faces the front, while pulling the right fist back to above the hip. When viewed from the front, the thumb side of the forearm of the blocking arm should be aligned with the edge of the body.

• Following the steps outlined above for the opposite side, practice performing middle-level inside-to-outside blocks using the right arm.

Points to remember

1) Upon completing the block, the elbow of the blocking arm should be bent at a 90-degree angle and the distance between the upper arm and the body should be roughly equivalent to the width of your fist. This should bring the fist of the blocking arm level with the shoulder.

2) When performing *uchi ude-uke*, the chest begins from a contracted position (as shown in step 1), but should be expanded fully when blocking.

Practicing chūdan uchi ude-uke 1

Stance: *Soto hachiji-dachi* (open V stance) to *zenkutsu-dachi* (front stance)

1) Stand in an open V stance with both arms extended downward in front of the body and the fists roughly shoulder-width apart.

2) Pull the right foot in toward the left foot and bend the knees while drawing the right fist to below the left underarm with the back of the hand facing upward. At the same time, extend the left arm out in front of the body.

3) With the feeling of pushing the left hand forward, advance the right foot one half-step, keeping the hips facing the front.

4) Advance the right foot the remaining half-step into a front stance while simultaneously performing a middle-level inside-to-outside block. When delivering the block, turn the hips 45 degrees to *hanmi*.

• Return to step 1 and repeat several times.

Points to remember

1) Although contracting and then expanding the chest enables the delivery of a powerful block, there is a tendency to lean back when performing *chūdan uchi ude-uke*. Keep the back straight and perpendicular to the floor.

2) When blocking, tighten the muscles along the side of the body below the armpit of the blocking arm.

1   2   3   4

Practicing chūdan uchi ude-uke 2

Stepping forward

Stance: *Zenkutsu-dachi* (front stance) to *zenkutsu-dachi*

1) Assume a left downward-block ready position standing in a left front stance with the hips at *hanmi* (45-degree angle to the front).

2) Keeping the left knee bent at the same angle, bring the right foot forward to beside the left foot while drawing the right fist across the chest to below the left underarm with the back of the hand facing upward. At the same time, extend the left arm out in front of the body.

3) Advance the right foot one half-step, keeping the hips facing the front.

4) Advance the right foot the remaining half-step into a front stance, simultaneously performing a middle-level inside-to-outside block while turning the hips 45 degrees to *hanmi*.

   • Following the steps outlined above for the opposite side, advance with the left leg while delivering a middle-level inside-to-outside block with the left arm. Proceed forward in the same manner for several steps.

5   6   7

Stepping back

5) (From a right front stance) Keeping the right knee bent at the same angle, bring the right foot back to beside the left foot. At the same time, draw the left fist across the chest to below the right underarm while extending the right arm out in front of the body.

6) Draw the right foot back one half-step, keeping the hips facing the front.

7) Draw the right foot back the remaining half-step into a front stance, delivering the inside-to-outside block while turning the hips 45 degrees to *hanmi*.

   • Following the steps outlined above for the opposite side, step back with the left leg while delivering an inside-to-outside block with the right arm. Continue stepping back in the same manner for several steps.

Kihon ippon kumite (Basic one-step *kumite*) 1 基本一本組手 (一)

In karate, *kumite* refers to the free exchange of offensive and defensive techniques with an opponent. Training for *kumite* begins with basic *yakusoku kumite*, or promise sparring, in which the attacking technique and target are predetermined, and progresses to *jiyū kumite*, or free sparring. While *kumite* training usually begins with *gohon kumite* (five-step *kumite*), the course outlined in this book begins with the basic techniques used in five-step *kumite* applied to basic one-step *kumite*.

Proper etiquette prior to practicing *kumite*

1) Defender (left) and attacker face each other standing in open V stances, shift into closed V stances, and bow once to each other. (A bow is also required upon completing a *kumite* exercise.)
2) Both defender and attacker then shift back into open V stances.
3) When practicing five-step or basic one-step *kumite*, the attacker steps back into a front stance while performing a downward block. The attacker, by taking a step back to get into position, is displaying courtesy to his opponent. At this time, the attacker must make sure that the distance between himself and the defender, called *maai*, would enable the attacker to take one step forward and deliver an offensive technique that would make physical contact with the defender. This is the ready position that the attacker must assume in preparation for practicing basic promise sparring.

1

2

3

Jōdan-zuki (Upper-level punch) 1

Block: *Jōdan age-uke* (Upper-level rising block) / ***Counterattack***: *Chūdan gyaku-zuki* (Middle-level reverse punch)

1) The attacker (right), stepping back into a left front stance, assumes a left down-ward-block ready position (*yōi*). / The defender stands in an open V stance.
2) The attacker steps forward and delivers a right upper-level lunge punch. / The defender steps back and blocks with a left upper-level rising block.
3) The defender counters with a right middle-level reverse punch.

Points to remember

1) The attacker must deliver a forceful attack with the intent of felling his opponent with a single strike.
2) When blocking, the defender must not pull his hips back in retreat, but should use the rotation of the hips to ensure a strong and effective block.

1

2

3

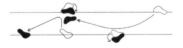

Chūdan-zuki (Middle-level punch) 1

Block: *Chūdan soto ude-uke* (Middle-level outside-to-inside block) / ***Counterattack***: *Chūdan gyaku-zuki* (Middle-level reverse punch)

1) The attacker (right), stepping back into a left front stance, assumes a left downward-block ready position (*yōi*). / The defender stands in an open V stance.

2) The attacker steps forward and delivers a right middle-level lunge punch. / The defender steps back and blocks with a left middle-level outside-to-inside block.

3) The defender counters with a right middle-level reverse punch.

1

2

3

LESSON **6**

- Lesson 5: Review (Approx. 30 min.)
- Chūdan shutō-uke (Middle-level knife-hand block) 1
- Kōkutsu-dachi (Back stance)
- Chūdan shutō-uke 2
- Yoko-geri kekomi (Side thrust kick)
- Gohon kumite (Five-step *kumite*)

Chūdan shutō-uke (Middle-level knife-hand block) 1 中段手刀受け (一)

In *chūdan shutō-uke*, the blocking hand, formed into *shutō* (knife hand), describes a gradually descending arc outward and the little-finger side of the hand is used to deflect punches to the chest area.

Chūdan shutō-uke: Overview of arm movements

1) Stand in an L stance (*renoji-dachi*) with the right foot in front of the left. Both hands are formed into the knife-hand position, the right hand pulled back to above the left shoulder with the back of the hand facing outward, the left hand extended out in front of the body.

2) Draw the right hand forward using the elbow as a pivot while pulling the left elbow back toward the body, gradually rotating the left hand so that the back of the hand begins to face outward.

3) Continue to draw the blocking arm around to the front of the body but keep the wrist locked until just before the block has been completed. At the same time, continue pulling the left elbow back while rotating the left hand.

4) Complete the block with a slicing motion of the right hand to deflect the attack to the side. Rotate the blocking hand at the moment of contact so that the back of the hand faces upward at a 45-degree angle. At the same time, pull the left elbow back, positioning the left hand in front of the solar plexus with the back of the hand facing downward and the fingers protruding just beyond the edge of the body.

1

2

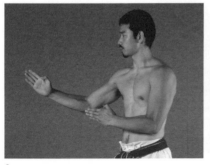

3

4

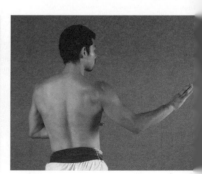

4 (rear-angle view)

Practicing chūdan shutō-uke 1

Stance: *Renoji-dachi* (L stance)

1) Stand in an L stance with the right foot in front of the left and the hips facing the front. Both hands are formed into the knife-hand position, with the right hand pulled back to above the left shoulder, the back of the hand facing outward, and the left hand extended out in front of the body.

2) Keeping the right wrist locked, draw the right hand forward, using the elbow as a pivot, while pulling the left elbow back toward the body. At the same time, gradually rotate the left hand so that the back of the hand begins to face outward.

3) Continue to draw the blocking arm around to the front of the body, keeping the wrist locked until just before the moment of contact. At the same time, continue pulling the left elbow back while rotating the left hand.

4) Complete the block with a slicing motion of the right hand while turning the hips 45 degrees to *hanmi*. Rotate the wrist of the blocking arm at the last moment so that the back of the hand faces upward at a 45-degree angle while drawing the left hand back to in front of the solar plexus.

Points to remember

1) To perform *shutō-uke* effectively, it is necessary to time the rotation of the hands properly. The pulling hand turns throughout the technique while the blocking hand does not begin turning until just before making contact.

2) When viewed from the front, the elbow of the blocking arm should not extend beyond the edge of the body. Additionally, when blocking, tighten the muscles along the side of the body below the armpit of the blocking arm.

1   2   3   4

Kōkutsu-dachi (Back stance) 後屈立ち

Kōkutsu-dachi, a stance that in no way resembles any posture that we normally assume in our everyday lives, plays a very important role in karate. The following exercises combine the practice of this stance with *chūdan shutō-uke* (middle-level knife-hand block).

1   2   3

Practicing kōkutsu-dachi

Stance: *Kōkutsu-dachi* (back stance) to *kōkutsu-dachi*

1) Assume a left middle-level knife-hand block ready position (*yōi*) standing in a right back stance (with the left foot in front of the right).

2) Turn the head to face the rear while drawing the right hand up to the left shoulder and extending the left arm to the rear at an angle.

3) Shift the center of gravity toward the left leg, moving into a left back stance facing the opposite direction, with the left leg supporting most of the body's weight. At the same time, deliver a right middle-level knife-hand block.

4) Turn the head to face the rear, pulling the left hand to above the right shoulder while extending the right arm to the rear at an angle.

4

• Shift the center of gravity toward the right leg, moving into a right back stance so that the right leg supports most of the body's weight. At the same time, deliver a left middle-level knife-hand block in the opposite direction, as in step 1.

Chūdan shutō-uke 2 中段手刀受け (二)

Stepping forward

Stance: *Kōkutsu-dachi* (back stance) to *kōkutsu-dachi*

1) Assume a left middle-level knife-hand block ready position (*yōi*) standing in a right back stance.
2) Keeping the right knee bent at the same angle, bring the right foot forward to beside the left foot while drawing the right hand up to the left shoulder and extending the left arm out in front of the body.
3) Advance the right foot one half-step, keeping the hips facing the front.
4) Advance the right foot the remaining half-step into a back stance while performing a right middle-level knife-hand block.

1   2   3   4

Stepping back

5) (From a left back stance) Keeping the left knee bent at the same angle, draw the right foot back to beside the left foot while pulling the left hand up to the right shoulder and extending the right arm out in front of the body.

6) Draw the right foot back one half-step, keeping the hips facing the front.

7) Draw the right foot back the remaining half-step into a back stance while performing a left middle-level knife-hand block.

Points to remember

1) Whether stepping forward or back, the hips should remain at the same height throughout; do not allow the hips to rise and fall with each step.

2) Do not lean back when performing *chūdan shutō-uke*; keep the upper body perpendicular to the floor throughout the exercise.

3) Both hands are formed into *shutō* (knife hand) throughout the exercise.

5   6   7

Yoko-geri kekomi (Side thrust kick) 横蹴り蹴こみ

In *yoko-geri kekomi*, also called *yoko-kekomi*, the edge of the foot (*sokutō*) is used to strike targets at various levels, including the face, chest, solar plexus, and knees. Side thrust kicks use the extension of the knee to deliver a powerful attack.

Practicing yoko-geri kekomi 1

Stance: *Heisoku-dachi* (Closed parallel stance)

1) Stand in a closed parallel stance with the fists out to the sides, the head turned facing the right, and the knees bent slightly.
2) Lift the right knee, bringing the foot up to beside the knee of the supporting leg.
3) Deliver a right side thrust kick, forcefully extending the leg out to the side. When kicking, thrust the hip in the direction of the target.
   - Upon delivering the kick, draw the leg back to the same position as step 2.
   - Return to the original ready position and repeat the exercise several times.

Points to remember

1) When kicking, do not allow the upper body to lean forward or too far to the side opposite to the target.
2) To ensure a powerful technique, turn the hips away from the direction of the kick while driving the foot toward the target.

1

2

3

Training method for beginning students

It is important for beginning students to understand how to deliver a thrust kick. The following exercise provides an easy means for these students to develop a feel for how to perform this type of kick.

1) Begin from a reclining position with the back against the floor, the head raised, and the hands clasped behind the head. Draw the right foot up toward the inside of the right thigh with the knee out to the right side. Extend the left leg out at an angle to the left side. Do not allow either leg to touch the floor.

2) Draw the left foot up toward the inside of the left thigh while extending the right leg. Direct the right foot out at an angle to the side while keeping the leg just above the floor.

3) Fully extend the right leg, thrusting the edge of the foot out at an angle to the right side while pulling the left foot in toward the inside of the left thigh.
   • Continue the exercise by performing a thrust kick with the left leg.

1

2

3

Practicing yoko-geri ke-age (side snap kick) 3

Stance: *Renoji-dachi (L stance) to kōkutsu-dachi (back stance)*

1) Stand in an L stance with the right foot in front of the left. The head is turned facing the right-hand side and the right fist is pulled back to the left hip, positioned on top of the left fist. The back of the left hand faces downward and the back of the right hand faces outward.

2) Without moving the upper body, raise the right foot to alongside the left knee in preparation for a right side snap kick.

3) Simultaneously deliver a right upper-level side snap kick to the right side along with a right upper-level side round back-fist strike in the same direction.

1   2   3

3 (side angle view)   4 (side angle view)   5

3b) Side-angle view of the simultaneous side snap kick and back-fist strike.

4) Turn the head to the left to face the opposite direction while pulling the kicking foot back toward the knee of the supporting leg. At the same time, pull the left hand, formed into a knife hand, up to above the right shoulder and thrust the right hand, also formed into a knife hand, out across the chest to the left side.

5) Plant the right foot to the rear, shifting into a right back stance while executing a left middle-level knife-hand block.

Points to remember

1) When performing *yoko-geri ke-age* (side snap kick), a snapping motion of the knee is used to deliver the kick, while in *yoko-geri kekomi* (side thrust kick), a thrusting motion is realized by forcefully extending the knee of the kicking leg. When practicing side kicks, it should be clear which type you are performing from the way in which the kicking leg is used.

2) Do not allow the hips to rise during the step preceding the delivery of the kick.

3) Use a snapping motion of the knee for an effective kick.

Gohon kumite (Five-step *kumite*) 五本組手

Gohon kumite is a form of *yakusoku kumite*, or promise sparring, in which two participants repeat the same fundamental attacking and blocking techniques for five consecutive steps. When practicing *gohon kumite*, the attacker must deliver each attack with the intent of felling his opponent with a single strike. Similarly, the defender must respond to each attack with a block powerful enough to eliminate the attacker's will to continue attacking.

Jōdan-zuki (Upper-level punch)

1) The attacker (right), stepping back into a left front stance, assumes a left downward-block ready position (*yōi*). / The defender stands in an open V stance.
2) The attacker steps forward and delivers a right upper-level lunge punch. / The defender steps back and blocks with a left upper-level rising block.
3) The attacker steps forward and delivers a left upper-level lunge punch. / The defender steps back and blocks with a right upper-level rising block.
4) Same as step 2.
5) Same as step 3.
6) Same as step 2. The attacker releases a *kiai* (a loud vocalization, such as "*yaah!*") with the final attack.
7) The defender counters with a right middle-level reverse punch while releasing a *kiai*.

After the counterattack, both the attacker and defender shift into *soto hachiji-dachi* (open V stances), the attacker by drawing the front foot back one half-step, and the defender by moving the rear foot forward one half-step. The defender, stepping back with the right foot into a left *gedan-barai* (downward block) ready position, then assumes the role of attacker, following the steps outlined above.

1

2

3

4

5

6

7

Chūdan-zuki (Middle-level punch)

1) The attacker (right), stepping back into a left front stance, assumes a left downward-block ready position (*yōi*). / The defender stands in an open V stance.

2) The attacker steps forward and delivers a right middle-level lunge punch. / The defender steps back and blocks with a left middle-level outside-to-inside block.

3) The attacker steps forward and delivers a left middle-level lunge punch. / The defender steps back and blocks with a right middle-level outside-to-inside block.

4) Same as step 2.

5) Same as step 3.

6) Same as step 2. The attacker releases a *kiai* (a loud vocalization, such as "*yaah!*") with the final attack.

7) The defender counters with a right middle-level reverse punch while releasing a *kiai.*

After the counterattack, both the attacker and defender shift into *soto hachiji-dachi* (open V stances), the attacker by drawing the front foot back one half-step, and the defender by moving the rear foot forward one half-step. The defender, stepping back with the right foot into a left *gedan-barai* (downward block) ready position, then assumes the role of attacker, following the steps outlined above.

1

2

3

②→③

4

③→④

5

④→⑤

6

⑤→⑥

7

The author performs a jumping side kick in response to Instructor Keinosuke Enoeda's powerful side thrust kick.

The author counters Instructor Enoeda's dynamic roundhouse kick with a back kick.

A driving front snap kick lifts the opponent into the air.

A side elbow strike is used to counter an opponent's punch.

CHAPTER 3

Kata, Basic Combination Techniques and Sparring Basics

Tettsui-uchi (Hammer-fist strike) 鉄槌打ち

Tettsui-uchi can be used to strike such targets as the head, face, solar plexus, and side of the body. To ensure an effective hammer-fist strike, use a snapping motion of the elbow and wrist. There are two types of hammer-fist strike, depending on the path that the arm travels: vertical round hammer-fist strike and side round hammer-fist strike.

Practicing tate-mawashi tettsui-uchi (Vertical round hammer-fist strike)

Stance: *Renoji-dachi* (L stance)

1) Stand in an L stance with the right foot in front of the left and the right arm extended in a downward block in the same direction as the right foot. The left hand is placed on the left hip. Swing the right fist up to above the head in an arcing motion centered on the elbow.

2) Using the elbow as a pivot, draw the fist down sharply with a snapping motion of the elbow and wrist. When completed, the fist should be level with the shoulder.

Points to remember

The effectiveness of *tettsui-uchi* depends on the snapping motion of the elbow and wrist at the moment of impact.

1

2

Practicing yoko-mawashi tettsui-uchi (Side round hammer-fist strike)

Stance: *Soto hachiji-dachi* (open V stance) to *kiba-dachi* (straddle-leg stance)

1) Stand in an open V stance with the head turned facing the right. The left arm is extended across the chest to the right with the hand open and the back of the hand facing upward. The right fist is pulled back below the left underarm with the thumb-side of the fist against the body.

2) With the feeling of pushing each hand farther out to each side, compress the chest while drawing the right foot out to the side one half-step.

3) Launch the right fist on an arcing path centered on the elbow so that the forearm travels on a plane parallel to the floor, using a snapping motion of the elbow and wrist while shifting into a straddle-leg stance. At the same time, pull the left fist back sharply to above the left hip and expand the chest fully to generate additional power.

1   2   3

Points to remember

1) When performing *yoko-mawashi tettsui-uchi*, do not allow the upper body to lean back upon completing the technique. Keep the back straight and perpendicular to the floor.

2) To ensure an effective *tettsui-uchi*, use a snapping motion of the elbow and wrist.

3) A strong *kiba-dachi* provides a solid foundation for delivering *tettsui-uchi*. Make sure that the stance is performed decisively and properly.

Kata: Heian Shodan 平安初段

A *kata* is a prearranged series of offensive and defensive techniques that is performed individually against multiple imaginary opponents. There are several important factors to remember when practicing *kata*, the first of which is that *kata* always begin and end with a bow. Also, *kata* must be performed with power, giving careful consideration to the overall flow and rhythm of techniques that make up each *kata*. Special attention must also be paid to three critical aspects of karate: muscle contraction and relaxation, the expansion and contraction of the body, and the speed with which techniques are performed. The *embusen*, or performance line, dictates the overall pattern of movements unique to each *kata* and must be strictly observed. And finally, even after completing a *kata*, it is necessary to maintain a state of physical and mental preparedness, called *zanshin*.

The Heian Shodan *kata*, made up of 21 movements, combines some of karate's most basic techniques—downward blocks, middle-level lunge punches, rising blocks, middle-level knife-hand blocks, and a hammer-fist strike. The *embusen* resembles the shape of the capital letter I, which facilitates the practice of the basic leg movements, or *unsoku*, employed in karate. As can be said of all *kata*, the practitioner—provided he carefully adheres to the *embusen* and all of the movements and stances are performed correctly—should finish performing Heian Shodan in the same location as where he began.

Practicing kata: Heian Shodan

Ready position (***yōi***): *Soto hachiji-dachi* (open V stance) with both fists positioned in front of the hips
  • Turn the head to the left while drawing the left foot out and to the rear. At the same time, pull the left fist up to above the right shoulder and thrust the right fist out at an angle toward the left.

1) *Hidari gedan-barai*
Shift into a left front stance facing the left side while performing a left downward block.

2) *Migi chūdan oi-zuki*
Step forward with the right foot into a right front stance while delivering a right middle-level lunge punch.
  • Turn the head to the right to view the rear while pulling the right foot back and across to the opposite side of the left foot, pivoting on the left foot to turn the body 180 degrees to the right. At the same time, pull the right fist up to above the left shoulder and thrust the left fist out at an angle toward the rear.

3) *Migi gedan-barai*
Shift into a right front stance facing the rear while performing a right downward block.

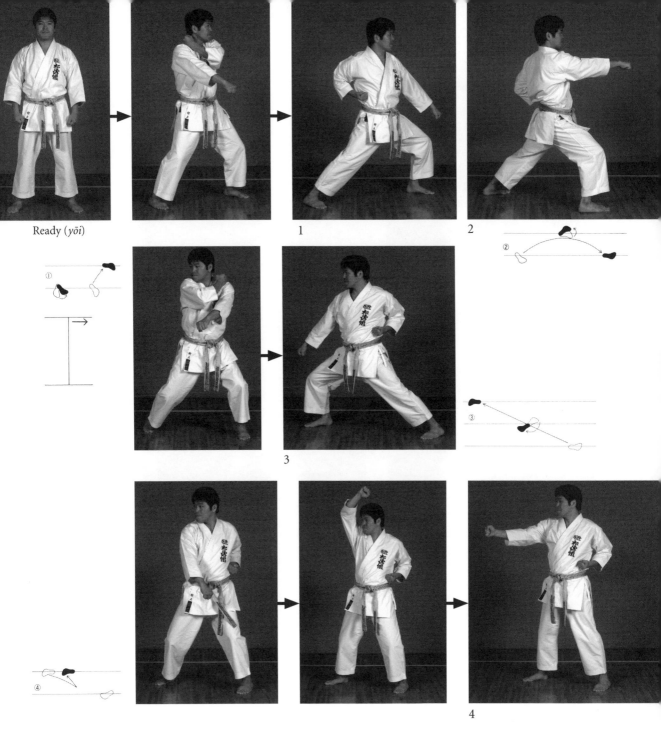

Ready (*yōi*)

1

2

3

4

- In response to an opponent grasping the right wrist, twist the wrist inward while pulling it back sharply to the front of the left hip. At the same time, draw the right hip inward while pulling the right foot back for greater momentum.
- Pull the right foot back one half-step, shifting into a right L stance, while swinging the right fist up to above the head in a large sweeping motion.

4) *Migi tate-mawashi tettsui-uchi*

Draw the right fist down sharply in a vertical round hammer-fist strike while standing in a right L stance.

5

6

5) *Hidari chūdan oi-zuki*

Step forward with the left foot into a left front stance while delivering a left middle-level lunge punch.

- Turn the head to the left (the same orientation as the original ready position) while pulling the left foot back, pivoting on the right foot to turn the body 90 degrees to the left. At the same time, pull the left fist up to above the right shoulder and thrust the right fist out at an angle toward the left.

6) *Hidari gedan-barai*

Shift into a left front stance facing the front while performing a left downward block.

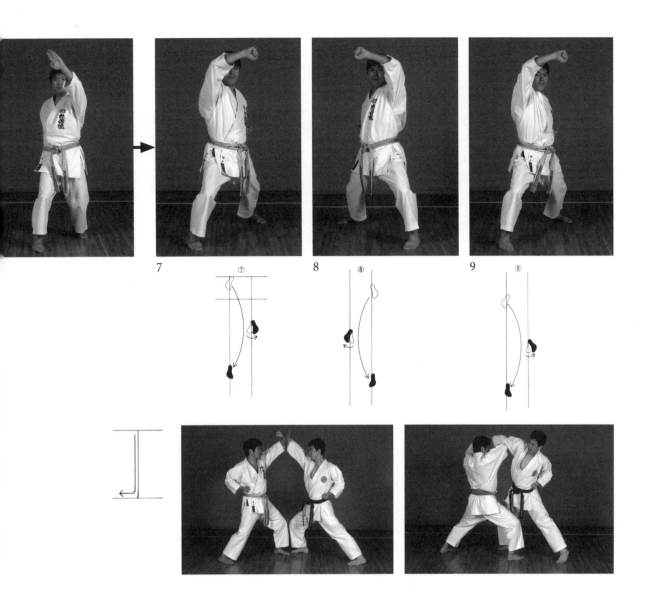

• Open the left hand and thrust it upward at an angle in front of the body.

7) *Migi jōdan age-uke*
Step forward with the right foot into a right front stance while performing a right upper-level rising block.

8) *Hidari jōdan age-uke*
Step forward with the left foot into a left front stance while performing a left upper-level rising block.

9) *Migi jōdan age-uke*
Step forward with the right foot into a right front stance while performing a right upper-level rising block with a *kiai* ("*eei!*").

10

11

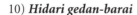

12

- Draw the left foot across the rear to the right side, pivoting on the right foot to turn the body 270 degrees to the left (to face toward the right side). At the same time, pull the left fist up to above the right shoulder and thrust the right fist out across the chest and below the left underarm.

10) *Hidari gedan-barai*
Shift into a left front stance facing the right side while performing a left downward block.

11) *Migi chūdan oi-zuki*
Step forward with the right foot into a right front stance while delivering a right middle-level lunge punch.

12) *Migi gedan-barai*
Pull the right foot back and across to the opposite side of the left foot, pivoting on the left foot to turn 180 degrees to the right into a right front stance while performing a right downward block.

13) *Hidari chūdan oi-zuki*
Step forward with the left foot into a left front stance while delivering a left middle-level lunge punch.

13

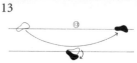

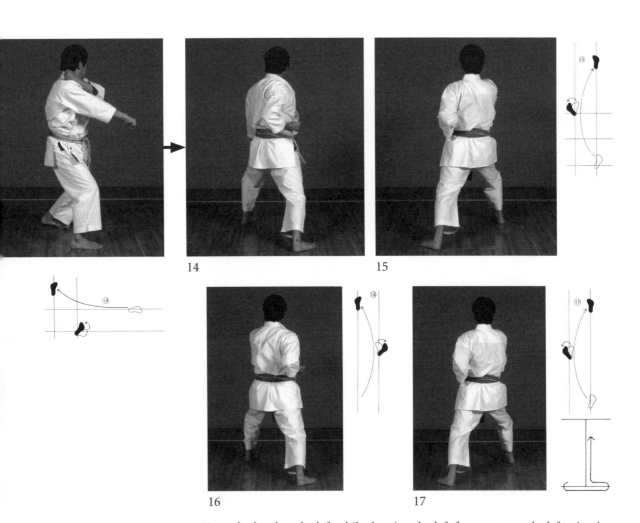

14

15

16

17

• Turn the head to the left while drawing the left foot across to the left, pivoting on the right foot to turn the body 90 degrees to the left. At the same time, pull the left fist up to above the right shoulder and thrust the right fist out at an angle toward the left.

14) *Hidari gedan-barai*
Shift into a left front stance facing the rear while performing a left downward block.

15) *Migi chūdan oi-zuki*
Returning down the center line of the *embusen*, step forward with the right foot into a right front stance while delivering a right middle-level lunge punch.

16) *Hidari chūdan oi-zuki*
Step forward with the left foot into a left front stance while delivering a left middle-level lunge punch.

17) *Migi chūdan oi-zuki*
Step forward with the right foot into a right front stance while delivering a right middle-level lunge punch with a *kiai* ("*yaah!*").

18

19

- Draw the left foot across the rear to the right side, pivoting on the right foot to turn the body 270 degrees to the left (to face toward the right side). At the same time, pull the left hand, formed into a knife hand, up to above the right shoulder and thrust the right hand, also formed into a knife hand, out across the chest and below the left underarm.

18) *Hidari chūdan shutō-uke*

Shift into a right back stance facing the right side while performing a left middle-level knife-hand block.

- Draw the right foot forward at a 45-degree angle to the right while pulling the right knife hand up to above the left shoulder and thrusting the left knife hand out in front of the solar plexus.

19) *Migi chūdan shutō-uke*

Shift into a left back stance while performing a right middle-level knife-hand block.

- Draw the right foot back at a 135-degree angle to the right while pulling the right knife hand up to above the left shoulder and thrusting the left knife hand out across the chest.

20

21

20) *Migi chūdan shutō-uke*

Shift into a left back stance while performing a right middle-level knife-hand block.

- Draw the left foot forward at a 135-degree angle to the left while pulling the left knife hand up to above the right shoulder and thrusting the right knife hand out in front of the solar plexus.

21) *Hidari chūdan shutō-uke*

Shift into a right back stance while performing a left middle-level knife-hand block.

Naore

(*Naore* is a command to return to a natural-posture stance.)

- Draw the left foot back, placing it beside the right foot in an open V stance. At the same time cross the arms in front of the chest.
- Extend the arms in front of the body so that the fists are positioned in front of the hips as in the original ready position. Maintain a state of physical and mental readiness (*zanshin*), prepared to respond to a potential attack, regardless of when or from where it may come.

Mawashi-geri (Roundhouse kick) 回し蹴り

In *mawashi-geri*, the ball of the foot (*koshi*) travels along a circular course from the outside to strike such targets as the head and the side of the body. The force driving a roundhouse kick is generated by the rotation of the hips and a snapping motion of the knee.

Practicing mawashi-geri 1

Stance: *Zenkutsu-dachi* (front stance)

1) Assume a left downward-block ready position (*yōi*) standing in a left front stance with the hips at *hanmi* (45-degree angle to the front).

2) Keeping the hips at *hanmi*, lift the right knee to the side of the body with the heel tucked tightly against the back of the right hip and the ball of the foot raised.

3) Deliver a right roundhouse kick, turning the hips in the direction of the kick and using the snapping motion of the knee. The foot travels along a large curving path around the body.

 • Immediately pull the right heel back to the hip.

 • Return the kicking foot to its original location on the floor and assume the initial ready position once again.

1   2   3

Training method for beginning students

The following exercise enables beginning students to practice the correct leg movement when performing a roundhouse kick, and to acquire the feel for using the ball of the foot to strike a target.

1) Begin from a reclining position with the left side of the body against the floor, the left arm extended straight out to the side and the right hand resting on the floor directly in front of the chest. The right knee is bent with the heel of the foot pressed against the back of the right hip and the knee pointing upward. From this position, the hips should be at *hanmi*, oriented at a 45-degree angle to the floor.
2) Using the knee as a pivot, draw the right foot up in a large arcing motion toward the front while turning the hips in the direction of the kick.
3) Follow through with the movement until the foot makes contact with the floor in front of the body, straightening the knee while strongly pressing the ball of the foot against the floor.
   • Return to the original starting position by performing the movements described in steps 2 and 3 in reverse.

At first, this exercise should be practiced slowly. Once you become more comfortable with the movement, gradually increase speed and use a snapping motion of the hips to generate additional power.

1

2

3

Practicing mawashi-geri 2

Stance: *Zenkutsu-dachi* (front stance) to *zenkutsu-dachi*

1) Stand in a left front stance with both arms extended down at an angle to the sides and the hips facing the front.

2) Lift the right knee to the side of the body with the heel tucked tightly against the back of the right hip. At the same time, turn the hips 45 degrees to the right so that they are at *hanmi*. Initially, grab the ankle with the right hand and pull the right heel back toward the hip.

3) Deliver a right roundhouse kick with the feeling of striking the target with the knee. Use the snapping motion of the knee and the turning of the hips to drive the foot from the outside in a large sweeping motion toward the target.

4) Immediately snap the kicking leg back with the feeling of kicking the back of the hip with the heel of the foot.

   • Step forward with the kicking leg into a right front stance and, following the steps outlined above for the opposite side, deliver a roundhouse kick with the left leg.

Points to remember

When lifting the knee prior to kicking and when pulling the leg back immediately after the kick, bend the knee of the supporting leg slightly to ensure that the motion of the kicking leg will not affect the ability to maintain proper balance.

1   2   3   4

Kihon (Basic) combinations 連続基本

Once the most fundamental punching, kicking, and blocking techniques have been learned and can be performed with some degree of proficiency, it is time to practice combination techniques, which combine offensive and defensive techniques into logical sequences that could be applied to actual sparring conditions. The following six exercises represent some of karate's most basic combination techniques.

Combination 1: Sanbon-zuki (Three-punch combination)

Stance: *Zenkutsu-dachi* (front stance) to *zenkutsu-dachi*

1) Assume a left downward-block ready position standing in a left front stance with the hips at *hanmi* (45-degree angle to the front).

2) *Migi jōdan oi-zuki*

   Step forward with the right foot into a right front stance while delivering a right upper-level lunge punch.

3) *Hidari chūdan gyaku-zuki*

   Pausing briefly, release all tension in the body immediately after completing the upper-level lunge punch, and then deliver a left middle-level reverse punch.

4) *Migi chūdan jun-zuki*

   Deliver a right middle-level front punch in rapid succession following the punch in the previous step.

1

2

3

4

5) *Hidari jōdan oi-zuki*

Step forward with the left foot into a left front stance while delivering a left upper-level lunge punch.

6) *Migi chūdan gyaku-zuki*

As in step 3, pause briefly, releasing all tension in the body, then deliver a right middle-level reverse punch.

7) *Hidari chūdan jun-zuki*

Deliver a left middle-level front punch in rapid succession following the previous punch.

• Once you become comfortable performing this combination, practice it while stepping backward instead of forward.

Points to remember

1) Even though this combination contains three punches in all, the initial punch must be delivered forcefully, with the intent of felling an opponent.

2) Rather than trying to propel the punching arm forward as fast as possible, focus on drawing the pulling arm back sharply and quickly. Doing so will enable the punch to be delivered with greater speed.

3) The positioning of the upper-level and middle-level targets must remain consistent throughout the exercise.

5

6

7

Combination 2: Age-uke (Rising block)—Gyaku-zuki (Reverse punch)

Stance: *Zenkutsu-dachi* (front stance) to *zenkutsu-dachi*

1) Assume a right downward-block ready position standing in a right front stance with the hips at *hanmi* (45-degree angle to the front).

2) Draw the left foot forward alongside the right foot while thrusting the right hand upward at an angle in front of the body.

3) ***Hidari jōdan age-uke***

   Step forward with the left foot into a left front stance while performing a left upper-level rising block.

4) ***Migi chūdan gyaku-zuki***

   Upon completing the block, immediately deliver a right middle-level reverse punch.

1

2

3

4

5   6   7

5) Draw the right foot forward alongside the left foot while thrusting the left hand upward at an angle in front of the body.

6) *Migi jōdan age-uke*

Step forward with the right foot into a right front stance while performing a right upper-level rising block.

7) *Hidari chūdan gyaku-zuki*

Upon completing the block, immediately deliver a left middle-level reverse punch.

• Once you become comfortable practicing this combination, perform it while stepping backward.

Points to remember

1) The rising block must be performed correctly and completely before delivering the reverse punch.

2) The hips are at *hanmi* when blocking, and turn to face squarely toward the front when punching. The rotation of the hips during this transition must be performed clearly.

Combination 3: Soto ude-uke (Outside-to-inside block)—Empi-uchi (Elbow strike)—Uraken-uchi (Backfist strike)

Stance: *Zenkutsu-dachi* (front stance) to *kiba-dachi* (straddle-leg stance)

1) Assume a left downward-block ready position standing in a left front stance with the hips at *hanmi* (45-degree angle to the front).

2) Draw the right foot forward alongside the left foot while pulling the right elbow back and out to the side, and the right fist up to beside the right ear. At the same time, extend the left arm out in front of the solar plexus.

3) ***Migi chūdan soto ude-uke***
   Step forward with the right foot into a right front stance while performing a right outside-to-inside block.

4) Draw the right foot back one half-step toward the left foot while extending the right arm across the chest toward the left and up at an angle. The right hand is formed into a knife hand with the palm facing up.

1

2

3

4

5

6

7

5) *Migi chūdan yoko empi-uchi*

Drive the right foot forward into a straddle-leg stance while delivering a right middle-level side elbow strike.

6) *Migi chūdan yoko-mawashi uraken-uchi*

Immediately following the elbow strike, deliver a right middle-level side round back-fist strike.

7) Draw the left foot forward alongside the right foot while pulling the left elbow back and the left fist to beside the left ear. At the same time, extend the right arm out in front of the solar plexus.

8

9

10

11

8–11) Follow steps 3 to 6 outlined above using the opposite side.

- Once you become comfortable performing this combination, practice it while stepping backward.

Points to remember

1) Each stance must be performed properly, clearly demonstrating which stance is being used.
2) When shifting from *zenkutsu-dachi* into *kiba-dachi*, thrust off the rear foot to propel the body in the direction of the elbow strike. This will result in the rear foot sliding into place just after the front foot has. This type of sliding motion of the feet is called *yori-ashi*.

Combination 4: Uchi ude-uke (Inside-to-outside block)— Kizami-zuki (Jab)—Gyaku-zuki (Reverse punch)

Stance: *Zenkutsu-dachi* (front stance) to *zenkutsu-dachi*

1) Assume a left downward-block ready position standing in a left front stance with the hips at *hanmi* (45-degree angle to the front).

2) Bring the right foot forward alongside the left foot while drawing the right fist across the chest to below the left underarm. At the same time, extend the left arm out in front of the solar plexus.

3) ***Migi chūdan uchi ude-uke***

Step forward with the right foot into a right front stance while performing a right inside-to-outside block.

4) ***Migi jōdan kizami-zuki***

Extend the blocking arm and drive the shoulder forward to deliver a right upper-level jab. The hips remain at *hanmi*.

1

2

3

4

5) *Hidari chūdan gyaku-zuki*

Upon completing the jab, immediately deliver a left middle-level reverse punch.

6) Bring the left foot forward alongside the right foot while drawing the punching hand (the left fist) across the chest to below the right underarm. At the same time, extend the the right arm out in front of the solar plexus.

7) *Hidari chūdan uchi ude-uke*

Step forward with the left foot into a left front stance while performing a left inside-to-outside block.

8–9) Follow steps 4 and 5 outlined above using the opposite side.

• This combination should also be practiced while stepping backward.

Note:

While *jōdan kizami-zuki*, a type of *jun-zuki* (front punch), is often used in *kumite* as a feint to distract an opponent's attention, it can also be used with great effectiveness as a decisive technique.

5

6

7

⑤→⑦

8

9

Combination 5: Shutō-uke (Knife-hand block)—Nukite (Spear hand)

Stance: *Kōkutsu-dachi* (back stance) to *zenkutsu-dachi* (front stance)

1) Assume a right middle-level knife-hand block ready position standing in a left back stance (with the right foot in front of the left).

2) Bring the left foot forward to beside the right foot while drawing the left hand, formed into a knife hand, up to the right shoulder. At the same time, extend the right arm out in front of the solar plexus with the right hand also formed into a knife hand.

3) ***Hidari chūdan shutō-uke***

   Step forward with the left foot into a right back stance while performing a left knife-hand block.

4) ***Migi chūdan nukite***

   Thrusting off the rear foot, shift into a left front stance by sliding the front foot out to the left while driving the right hand forward to deliver a right middle-level spear hand.

1

2

3

4

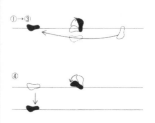

5) Bring the right foot forward alongside the left foot while drawing the right hand up to the left shoulder and extending the left arm out in front of the solar plexus.

6) *Migi chūdan shutō-uke*

Step forward with the right foot into a left back stance while performing a right knife-hand block.

7) *Hidari chūdan nukite*

Thrust off the rear foot and shift into a right front stance by sliding the front foot out to the right while delivering a left middle-level spear hand.

• This combination should also be practiced while stepping backward.

Points to remember

1) The transition between stances must be performed correctly, making clear which stance is being used during each stage of the combination.

2) The *nukite* strike could be thought of as a middle-level reverse punch executed with the hand formed into a knife hand instead of a fist.

5

6

7

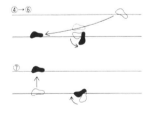

Combination 6: Ren-geri (Consecutive kicks)

Stance: *Zenkutsu-dachi* (front stance) to *zenkutsu-dachi*

1) Assume a left front stance with both arms extended down at an angle to the sides and the hips facing the front.
2) Lift the right knee, drawing the right foot up to beside the left knee.
3) ***Migi chūdan mae-geri***

   Deliver a right middle-level front snap kick.
   - Upon pulling the kicking leg back, step forward into a right front stance and lift the left knee, bringing the left foot up alongside the right knee.
4) ***Hidari jōdan mae-geri***

   Deliver a left upper-level front snap kick.
   - Retract the kicking leg and step forward into a left front stance.

Points to remember

1) The length of the front stance (the distance between the feet when viewed from the side) following the middle-level front snap kick should be slightly shorter than in a standard front stance.
2) The two kicks should be performed as a single flowing motion.

1   2   3   4

- Lesson 8: Review (Approx. 30 min.)
- Shutō-uchi (Knife-hand strike)
- Jūji-uke (X-block)
- Kihon ippon kumite (Basic one-step kumite) 2

Shutō-uchi (Knife-hand strike) 手刀打ち

In *shutō-uchi*, which can be used in attacks to the carotid arteries (on either side of the neck) and the side of the body, the outer edge of the hand strikes the target in a slicing motion. There are two types of knife-hand strike, depending on the path that the arm travels: outside round knife-hand strike and inside round knife-hand strike.

Practicing shutō-uchi

The following exercise combines both types of knife-hand strike in a single practice routine.

Stance: A slightly shortened *zenkutsu-dachi* (front stance)

1. Soto-mawashi shutō-uchi (Outside round knife-hand strike)

1) Stand in a slightly shortened left front stance with the left arm extended forward and the hand positioned in front of the solar plexus. The right elbow is pulled back to the side and the right hand, formed into a knife hand, is positioned beside the right ear with the palm facing outward. The hips are at *hanmi* (45-degree angle to the front).

2) Using the shoulder as a pivot, launch the right hand on a circular course around the body while turning the hips toward the front and pulling the left elbow back.

1

2

3) Complete the strike with a snapping motion of the elbow, driving the striking hand toward the target from the outside while turning the hips slightly beyond the point where they squarely face the front. Rotate the wrist of the striking arm just before contact is made so that the palm of the hand faces upward. At the same time, pull the left fist back sharply to above the left hip.

3

2. Uchi-mawashi shutō-uchi (Inside round knife-hand strike)

4) Draw the right hand (which has just completed the outside round knife-hand strike) back to above the left shoulder with the back of the hand facing outward. The hips face toward the front.

4

5) Launch the right hand outward on a circular course centered on the elbow while turning the hips to *gyaku-hanmi* (45-degree angle to the front, with the hip on the side opposite to the front leg pushed forward).

5

6) Complete the strike with a snapping motion of the elbow, turning the hips fully to *gyaku-hanmi*. Rotate the wrist of the striking arm as the knife hand approaches the target so that the back of the hand faces upward.

• Return to the original ready position and repeat the exercise several times.

6

Points to remember

1) The effectiveness of a *shutō-uchi* attack depends on the turning of the hips and the snapping motion of the elbow.

2) Using the pulling hand to add momentum to the turning of the hips will result in a more powerful technique.

3) When performing *shutō-uchi*, it is important to keep the thumb of the striking hand tightly locked against the edge of the hand.

Jūji-uke (X-block) 十字受け

Jūji-uke, formed by crossing the hands at the wrists, can be used with both hands either open or closed to defend against upper-level punches, as well as with the hands closed into fists against lower-level kicks. When performing *jōdan* (upper level) *jūji-uke*, the arms are thrust upward and the backs of either the open hands or fists are used to deflect attacks to the face. *Gedan* (lower level) *jūji-uke*, performed with the feeling of delivering a striking technique, is used to block kicking attacks.

Jōdan haishu jūji-uke (upper-level back-hand X-block) is performed with the hands open. As such, the attacker's punching arm can easily be grabbed after blocking, creating an opportunity for the defender to pull the attacker off-balance and respond with an effective counterattack.

When blocking a kick with *gedan seiken jūji-uke* (downward fist X-block), the crossed fists are thrust sharply against the attacker's shin, serving not only to block the attack but also doubling as a forceful counterattack.

1

Practicing jōdan haishu jūji-uke

Stance: *Zenkutsu-dachi* (front stance)

1) Stand in a left front stance with both fists pulled back to above the hips.
2) Drive both fists upward, crossing the arms at the wrists in front of the chest with the right hand positioned inside, between the left hand and the chest. Halfway through the block, the backs of the hands face the front.
3) Complete the block by extending both arms upward at an angle while opening the hands and rotating the wrists to "trap" the attacker's punch between the backs of the hands.

2

Points to remember

To ensure an effective block, it is necessary to use a snapping motion of the elbows and thrust off the rear leg to drive the hips forward.

3

Practicing gedan seiken jūji-uke

Stance: A shortened *zenkutsu-dachi* (front stance)

1) Stand in a shortened left front stance, with the front foot positioned roughly one half-step back from where it would be in a standard front stance, and the hips at *hanmi* (45-degree angle to the front). The fists, thumb-side up, are pulled back to above the right hip with the right fist above the left and the wrists crossed.

2) Advance the front leg forward one half-step while turning the hips toward the front. Use the rotation of the hips to launch the fists downward at an angle in front of the body.

3) Complete the block by extending the arms to drive the fists down, thumb-side up, while shifting into a full front stance with the hips facing the front. The left fist travels along a curved path centered on the elbow while the right fist travels in an almost straight line.

1   2   3

Points to remember

1) There is a tendency to lean forward when performing *gedan seiken jūji-uke*; keep the back straight and perpendicular to the floor.

2) To perform the technique correctly, extend both arms fully to complete the block.

3) The effectiveness of *gedan seiken jūji-uke* depends on the turning of the hips and the snapping motion of the elbow.

Kihon Ippon Kumite (Basic one-step kumite) 2 基本一本組手 (二)

Jōdan-zuki (Upper-level punch) 2

Block: *Jōdan tate shutō-uke* (Upper-level vertical knife-hand block) / ***Counterattack***:*Jōdan soto-mawashi shutō-uchi* (Upper-level outside round knife-hand strike)

1) The attacker (right) assumes a left downward-block ready position (*yōi*) standing in a left front stance. / The defender stands in an open V stance.

2) The attacker steps forward and delivers a right upper-level lunge punch. / The defender steps back with the right leg at a 45-degree angle to the right into a right back stance while blocking with a left upper-level vertical knife-hand block. At the same time, the right hand, also formed into a knife hand, is drawn back to beside the right ear in preparation for the counterattack.

3) The defender thrusts off the rear foot, shifting into a left front stance while countering with a right upper-level outside round knife-hand strike.

Points to remember

1) When executing the vertical knife-hand block, sharply pull the right knife hand back to beside the right ear, utilizing the power generated by expanding the chest for a more effective block.

2) When delivering the outside round knife-hand strike, use the rotation of the hips and draw the pulling hand back strongly to ensure a powerful technique.

1

2

3

Jōdan-zuki 3

Block: *Jōdan haishu jūji-uke* (Upper-level back-hand X-block) / **Counterattack**: *Chūdan mawashi-geri* (Middle-level roundhouse kick), *Chūdan ushiro-mawashi empi-uchi* (Middle-level back round elbow strike)

1) The attacker (right) assumes a left downward-block ready position (*yōi*) standing in a left front stance. / The defender stands in an open V stance.

2) The attacker steps forward and delivers a right upper-level lunge punch. / The defender steps straight back with the right leg into a left front stance while blocking with an upper-level back-hand X-block. When executing the block, the right hand is positioned above the left hand.

3) The defender firmly grasps the attacker's wrist with his right hand, pulling the defender forward to throw him off-balance while countering with a right middle-level roundhouse kick.

4) The defender immediately retracts the kicking leg after the kick.

5) The defender steps forward at an angle to the left with the kicking leg, planting the foot on the far side of the attacker's front leg while rotating the upper body to the left into a left front stance facing the opposite direction. At the same time, the defender delivers a left middle-level back round elbow strike.

Points to remember

1) When delivering the roundhouse kick, the stronger the attacker's arm is pulled forward, the more effective the kick will be.

2) Use the rotation of the upper body to generate momentum when delivering the back round elbow strike.

1

2

3

4

5

Chūdan-zuki 3

Block: *Gedan-barai* (Downward block) / *Counterattack*: *Jōdan yoko-geri ke-age* (Upper-level side snap kick), *Jōdan uchi-mawashi shutō-uchi* (Upper-level inside round knife-hand strike)

1) The attacker (right) assumes a left downward-block ready position (*yōi*) standing in a left front stance. / The defender stands in an open V stance.

2) The attacker steps forward and delivers a right middle-level lunge punch. / The defender shifts his body out of the path of the attack (*tai-sabaki*), stepping to the right side and back slightly while blocking with a downward block.

3) Upon blocking, the defender counters with a left upper-level side snap kick.

4) The defender steps toward the attacker with the kicking leg into a left front stance while simultaneously delivering a left upper-level inside round knife-hand strike.

Points to remember

1) When using *tai-sabaki* to evade an attack, it is necessary to take into account the counterattack to be used to determine the proper distance between yourself and your opponent (*maai*). Move the right foot out first, immediately followed by the left foot.

2) Utilize the forward momentum of the body when stepping forward after the kick to deliver a powerful knife-hand-strike counterattack.

Mae-geri (Front snap kick) 1

Block: *Gedan-barai* (Downward block) / ***Counterattack***: *Chūdan gyaku-zuki* (Middle-level reverse punch)

1) The attacker (right) stands in a left front stance with the fists out to the sides. / The defender stands in an open V stance.
2) The attacker steps forward and delivers a right middle-level front snap kick. / The defender steps straight back with the right leg into a left front stance while blocking with a left downward block.
3) The defender counters with a right middle-level reverse punch.

1

2

3

Points to remember

1) When blocking with a downward block, while there is a tendency to pull the hips back in retreat, it is essential that the hips remain forward to ensure an effective block.
2) After blocking, fully rotate the hips so they squarely face forward upon delivering the reverse punch. The orientation of the hips must be made clear for each technique, with the hips at *hanmi* (45-degree angle to the front) when blocking, and facing forward for the reverse punch.

Mae-geri 2

Block: *Gedan seiken jūji-uke* (Downward fist X-block) / **Counterattack**: *Jōdan shutō jūji-uchi* (Upper-level knife-hand X-strike)

1) The attacker (right) stands in a left front stance with the fists out to the sides. / The defender stands in an open V stance.
2) The attacker steps forward and delivers a right middle-level front snap kick. / The instant that the attacker begins to deliver the kick, the defender steps straight back with the left leg into a right front stance while blocking with a lower-level fist X-block.
3) Immediately after blocking, the defender draws the elbows back toward the body, keeping the wrists crossed and the fists aimed at the attacker's face.
4) The defender thrusts forward off the rear foot and counters with an upper-level knife-hand X-strike to the attacker's neck.

Points to remember

1) Timing is of critical importance when blocking with an X-block.
2) Make use of the attacker's forward momentum when delivering the X-strike to ensure a more effective counterattack.

Yoko-geri kekomi (Side thrust kick) 1

Block: *Gyaku gedan-barai* (Reverse downward block) / ***Counterattack***: *Jōdan kizami-zuki* (Upper-level jab), *Chūdan gyaku-zuki* (Middle-level reverse punch)

1) The attacker (right) stands in a left front stance with the fists out to the sides. / The defender stands in an open V stance.

2) The attacker steps forward and delivers a right middle-level side thrust kick. / The defender steps back and to the left with the right leg into a left front stance while blocking with a right reverse downward block with the hips at *gyaku-hanmi* (45-degree angle to the front, with the hip on the side opposite to the front leg pushed forward).

3) The defender counters with a left upper-level jab, rotating the hips to *hanmi*.

4) The defender follows through with a right middle-level reverse punch, rotating the hips so they squarely face forward.

1 2 3 4

Points to remember

1) To ensure an effective block, it is necessary to draw the pulling hand back sharply and make use of the rotation of the hips, turning them strongly to *gyaku-hanmi*.

2) Special attention must be paid to the use of the hips for each technique, making clear the *gyaku-hanmi* position during the reverse downward block, the *hanmi* position for the jab, and the front-facing position for the reverse punch.

The author performing parts of his own kata at the 1977 I.A.K.F World Championships.

A simultaneous side kick and back-fist strike combination.

A back round elbow strike is used in response to Instructor Keinosuke Enoeda's lunge punch.

Demonstrating a lunge punch before a class of 1,000 students during an outdoor training session in Tokyo.

CHAPTER 4

Arm-Leg Combinations, Kata and Basic Free-Sparring

Arm/Leg Kihon (Basic) combinations 天地連続基本

The *kihon* combinations presented in Lesson 8 consisted of sequences of either arm techniques or leg techniques. The following exercises combine both kicking and punching techniques.

Combination 1: Mae-geri (Front snap kick)—Oi-zuki (Lunge punch)

Stance: *Zenkutsu-dachi* (front stance) to *zenkutsu-dachi*

1) Assume a left downward-block ready position standing in a left front stance with the hips at *hanmi* (45-degree angle to the front).

2) *Migi jōdan mae-geri*
   Keeping both arms in place, deliver a right upper-level front snap kick.

3) Maintain the downward-block position of the arms until the kicking leg has been completely retracted.

4) *Migi chūdan oi-zuki*
   Step forward with the right foot into a right front stance while delivering a right middle-level lunge punch.

5) *Hidari jōdan mae-geri*
   Keeping both arms in place, deliver a left upper-level front snap kick.

6) Maintain the position of the arms until the kicking leg has been completely retracted.

7) *Hidari chūdan oi-zuki*
   Step forward with the left foot into a left front stance while delivering a left middle-level lunge punch.

Points to remember

1) By keeping the arms in place until the kicking leg has been pulled back after each kick, the subsequent momentum generated when stepping forward can be applied to the delivery of a powerful punching technique.

2) There is a tendency to lean forward when delivering a lunge punch immediately after a kick; keep the back straight and perpendicular to the floor.

1

2

3

4

5

6

7

Combination 2: Mae-geri (Front snap kick)— Gyaku-zuki (Reverse punch)

Stance: *Zenkutsu-dachi* (front stance) to *zenkutsu-dachi*

1) Assume a right middle-level reverse-punch ready position standing in a left front stance with the hips facing the front.

2) *Migi jōdan mae-geri*

   Keeping both arms in place, deliver a right upper-level front snap kick.

3) Maintain the position of the arms until the kicking leg has been completely retracted.

4) *Hidari chūdan gyaku-zuki*

   Step forward with the right foot into a right front stance while delivering a left middle-level reverse punch.

5) *Hidari jōdan mae-geri*

   Keeping both arms in place, deliver a left upper-level front snap kick.

6) Maintain the position of the arms until the kicking leg has been completely retracted.

7) *Migi chūdan gyaku-zuki*

   Step forward with the left foot into a left front stance while delivering a right middle-level reverse punch.

Points to remember

1) When kicking, it is important to tighten the abdominal muscles on the same side as the kicking leg to ensure that the corresponding shoulder does not rise.

2) The completion of each reverse punch should coincide with the planting of the kicking foot on the floor. This enables the forward momentum of the body after the kick to be applied to the delivery of a powerful punching technique.

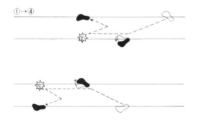

1   2

3   4

5   6

7

Ushiro-geri (Back kick) 後ろ蹴り

Ushiro-geri, for attacks to the rear, can be used to strike such targets as the face and solar plexus. The kicking leg is extended sharply backward in a thrusting motion and the heel of the foot (*kakato*) is used as the striking surface.

Practicing ushiro-geri 1

Stance: *Heisoku-dachi* (closed parallel stance)

1) Assume a closed parallel stance with the arms extended downward to the sides. Look over the right shoulder toward the rear.
2) Lift the right knee, drawing the right foot alongside the left knee. The sole of the kicking foot should be parallel to the floor, as when preparing to deliver a front snap kick.
3) Deliver a right back kick, thrusting the heel of the foot straight back by sharply extending the leg.
   - Upon delivering the kick, draw the leg back to the same position as step 2.
   - Return to the initial ready position and turn the head to look over the left shoulder toward the rear.

1   2   3

4   5

4) Lift the left knee, bringing the left foot up to beside the right knee.

5) Deliver a left back kick, driving the heel of the foot straight back.

   • After the kick, draw the leg back to the same position as step 4.

   • Return to the original ready position from step 1 and repeat the exercise several
     times.

Points to remember

1) Lift the knee of the kicking leg prior to the kick in the same manner as when
   preparing to deliver a front snap kick.

2) When performing *ushiro-geri*, there is a tendency for the upper body to "open
   up" in the direction of the kick. Deliver the kick with the feeling of pushing
   forward (away from the target) the shoulder on the same side of the body as
   the kicking leg.

3) Keep the supporting leg bent slightly throughout the technique.

4) Retract the kicking leg after the kick with the feeling of driving the knee forward.

Practicing ushiro-geri 2

Stance: *Zenkutsu-dachi* (front stance) to *zenkutsu-dachi*

1) Assume a left downward-block ready position standing in a left front stance with
   the hips at *hanmi* (45-degree angle to the front).

2) Pivoting on the front foot, rotate the hips 90 degrees to the right while drawing
   the rear foot roughly one half-step toward the front foot. A straight line pass-
   ing directly beneath the feet should coincide with the location of the target. The
   front knee (left knee) remains bent at the same angle so the hips do not rise, and
   the left arm stays extended in a downward block to the front. Look over the left
   shoulder to confirm the location of the target.

1   2   3   4

3) Lift the right foot, pointing the heel toward the target.

4) Deliver a right back kick, looking past the right shoulder toward the target.

5) Retract the kicking leg while turning to the right to face the front. At the same time, pull the right fist to above the left shoulder and thrust the left fist toward the front.

6) Step forward with the right foot into a right front stance while performing a right downward block.

7) Using the front foot as a pivot, turn the hips 90 degrees to the left while drawing the rear foot about one half-step toward the front foot. The hips remain at the same height and the right arm stays extended in a downward block to the front. Look over the right shoulder in the direction of the target.

8) Lift the left foot in preparation for the kick.

5   6   7   8

9

10

11

9) Deliver a left back kick, looking past the left shoulder toward the target.

10) Pull the kicking leg back while turning to the left, toward the front. At the same time, pull the left fist to above the right shoulder and thrust the right fist toward the front.

11) Step forward with the left foot into a left front stance while performing a left downward block.

Points to remember

1) The hips remain at the same height throughout the entire sequence of moves.

2) This technique requires that the body turn around to face the front immediately after kicking. In anticipation of this motion, there is a tendency for the upper body to "open up" during the kick. Accordingly, special care must be taken to ensure that the kick is delivered properly.

Mikazuki-geri (Crescent kick) 三日月蹴り

Mikazuki-geri, a kicking technique performed with a sweeping motion of the leg, offers both offensive and defensive applications. The ball of the foot (*koshi*) or the sole of the foot (*sokutei*) can be used to strike such targets as the solar plexus, abdomen, and groin, while the sole of the foot can be used to deflect an opponent's punch.

Practicing mikazuki-geri

Stance: *Kiba-dachi* (straddle-leg stance)

1) Stand in a straddle-leg stance with the head turned facing the left and the left arm extended directly out to the side. The left hand is open and level with the shoulder while the right fist is drawn back to above the hip.
2) Draw the right foot up across the front of the body to strike the palm of the left hand with the sole of the foot. Keep the left hand at the same height throughout the technique.
   • Immediately return to the original starting position by retracting the kicking foot along the same course it traveled to deliver the kick.

Points to remember

1) Unlike almost all of the kicks previously introduced, *mikazuki-geri* does not involve a snapping motion of the knee. Instead, the entire leg is swung around to drive the foot along a circular path toward the target.
2) When practicing *mikazuki-geri*, use the sole of the foot to strike the palm of the hand. Using the ball of the foot could result in injury to the hand.
3) When kicking, do not make any special effort to turn the upper body in the direction of the kick; concentrate only on generating momentum by swinging the leg toward the target.

1

2

LESSON 11

- Lesson 10: Review (Approx. 30 min.)
- Haiwan-uke (Back-arm block)
- Kata: Heian Nidan
- Ura-zuki (Close punch)

Haiwan-uke (Back-arm block) 背腕受け

In *haiwan-uke*, the upper surface of the forearm is used to defend against upper-level and middle-level punching and kicking attacks. Back-arm blocks include inside-to-outside and outside-to-inside blocks.

Practicing chūdan soto (middle-level outside-to-inside) haiwan-uke

Stance: *Soto hachiji-dachi* (open V stance) to *zenkutsu-dachi* (front stance)

1) Stand in an open V stance with both fists positioned in front of the hips.
2) Step back with the left foot into right front stance while drawing the right arm around from the outside along a circular path. Just before the moment of impact, rotate the forearm so that the upper surface of the forearm (*haiwan*) faces the direction of the block. At the same time, pull the left fist back sharply to above the left hip and turn the hips 45 degrees to *hanmi*.
   • Return to the original starting position and repeat the exercise several times.

Points to remember

When performing *chūdan soto haiwan-uke*, the elbow of the blocking arm should be bent slightly. Bending the elbow too much, however, will lessen the effectiveness of the block and could lead to injury.

1

2

Kata: Heian Nidan 平安二段

The Heian Nidan *kata*, comprising a total of 26 movements, combines a wide range of techniques: inside-to-outside back-arm blocks, hammer-fist strikes, close punches, front punches, a side snap kick, a back-fist strike, knife-hand blocks, a spear hand, reverse inside-to-outside blocks, front snap kicks, reverse punches, an augmented block, downward blocks, and rising blocks. Like Heian Shodan, the *embusen* (performance line) resembles the shape of the capital letter I.

Many of the techniques in Heian Nidan are performed while standing in back stances, providing an opportunity for karate students to practice what is for many a difficult stance to master. Additionally, the *kata* includes several combination techniques: a side snap kick and back-fist strike followed by a middle-level knife-hand block, and a front snap kick followed by a reverse punch. Accordingly, Heian Nidan is a *kata* that requires much practice to be performed well.

Practicing kata: Heian Nidan

Ready position (*yōi*): *Soto hachiji-dachi* (open V stance) with both fists positioned in front of the hips.

- Turn the head to the left and, leaving the fists in place, draw the left foot out to the left side.

1) ***Hidari jōdan uchi haiwan-uke***

Shift into a right back stance facing the left side while pulling both arms up in a sharp whipping motion to perform a left upper-level inside-to-outside back-arm block. The right arm, by moving in synchronization with the left, serves to provide additional momentum to the block, making possible a more powerful technique. In the completed position, the arms should describe a large horizontally oriented rectangle.

Ready (*yōi*)

1

2) **Migi jōdan tettsui-uchi (Migi chūdan ura-zuki)**

In response to an opponent's punch to the face, draw the left fist back toward the right shoulder to deflect the attack, rotating the wrist so that the back of the fist faces outward upon completing the block. At the same time, launch the right fist on a small circular course downward at an angle from the outside inward to deliver a right upper-level hammer-fist strike.

3) **Hidari chūdan zuki**

Extend the left arm sharply to the left to deliver a left middle-level punch while pulling the right fist back to above the right hip.

• Turn the head to the right to face the rear while driving the right fist across the body to the left and lowering the left fist slightly.

4) **Migi jōdan uchi haiwan-uke**

Transfer the center of gravity toward the left leg to assume a left back stance while swinging both arms up to perform a right upper-level inside-to-outside back-arm block.

2

3

4

5) *Hidari jōdan tettsui-uchi*

Draw the right fist back toward the left shoulder while delivering a left upper-level hammer-fist strike.

6) *Migi chūdan zuki*

Deliver a right middle-level punch to the right while pulling the left fist back to above the left hip.

· Turn the head to the right and move the rear foot one half-step toward the front foot. At the same time, pull the right fist back to the left side of the body, positioning it on top of the left fist with the thumb-side of the fist facing upward.

7) *Migi jōdan yoko-keage/Migi jōdan yoko-mawashi uraken-uchi*

Deliver a right upper-level side snap kick to the right side simultaneously with a right upper-level side round back-fist strike in the same direction.

5

6

7a

7b

• Turn the head to the left to face the opposite side (the same orientation as the original ready position) while pulling back the kicking leg. At the same time, pull the left hand, formed into a knife hand, up to above the right shoulder and thrust the right hand, also formed into a knife hand, out across the chest to the left side.

8) *Hidari chūdan shutō-uke*

Plant the right foot to the rear, shifting into a right back stance facing the front while performing a left middle-level knife-hand block.

9) *Migi chūdan shutō-uke*

Step forward with the right foot into a left back stance while performing a right middle-level knife-hand block.

10) *Hidari chūdan shutō-uke*

Step forward with the left foot into a right back stance while performing a left middle-level knife-hand block.

11

12

• In response to an opponent's middle-level punch, drop the left hand along a circular course centered on the elbow to perform a pressing block (*osae-uke*) while drawing the right foot forward.

11) **Migi chūdan nukite**

Step forward with the right foot into a right front stance while delivering a right middle-level spear hand with a *kiai* ("*yaah!*"). The left hand is positioned beneath the right arm for added support.

• Pull the left foot across the rear to the right side, pivoting on the right foot to turn the body 270 degrees to the left (to face the right side). At the same time, pull the left hand, formed into a knife hand, up to above the right shoulder and thrust the right hand, also formed into a knife hand, out across the chest and below the left underarm.

12) **Hidari chūdan shutō-uke**

Shift into a right back stance facing the right side while performing a left middle-level knife-hand block.

13

14

15

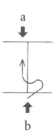

- Draw the right foot forward at a 45-degree angle to the right while pulling the right knife hand up to above the left shoulder and thrusting the left knife hand out in front of the body.

13) **Migi chūdan shutō-uke**

Shift into a left back stance while performing a right middle-level knife-hand block.

- Draw the right foot back to turn the body 135 degrees to the right while pulling the right knife hand up to above the left shoulder and thrusting the left knife hand out across the chest.

a

b

14) *Migi chūdan shutō-uke*

Shift into a left back stance while performing a right middle-level knife-hand block.

• Draw the left foot forward at a 45-degree angle to the left while pulling the left knife hand up to above the right shoulder and thrusting the right knife hand out in front of the body.

15) *Hidari chūdan shutō-uke*

Shift into a right back stance while performing a left middle-level knife-hand block.

• Turn the head to the left and draw the left foot across to the left, turning the body 45 degrees in the same direction (so as to look down the center line of the *embusen* from the end opposite to the original starting position). At the same time, swing the right arm back at an angle to the right in a large sweeping motion. The left arm remains in the same knife-hand-block position relative to the upper body.

• Transfer the center of gravity toward the left leg while swinging the right arm across the front of the body and below the right underarm.

16) *Migi chūdan gyaku uchi-uke*

Assume a slightly shortened left front stance while performing a right middle-level reverse inside-to-outside block, turning the hips to *gyaku hanmi* (45-degree angle to the front, with the hip on the side opposite to the front leg pushed forward).

a   b   16a   16b

17a

17b

18a

18b

17) **Migi jōdan mae-geri**

Keeping the arms in place, deliver a right upper-level front snap kick.

18) **Hidari chūdan gyaku-zuki**

Step forward with the right foot into a right front stance while delivering a left middle-level reverse punch.

- Extend the right arm straight out in front of the body while drawing the left fist across the chest to below the right underarm with the back of the fist facing upward.

19) **Hidari chūdan gyaku uchi-uke**

Perform a left middle-level reverse inside-to-outside block while turning the hips to *gyaku hanmi*. As the hips turn, the front foot moves back slightly but the front knee remains bent at the same angle.

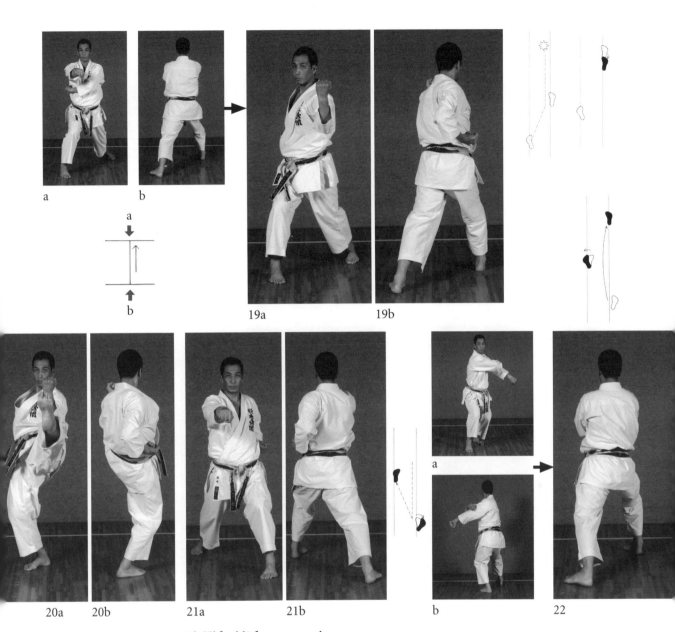

a   b

a
b

19a   19b

20a   20b   21a   21b   a   b   22

20) **Hidari jōdan mae-geri**

Keeping the arms in place, deliver a left upper-level front snap kick.

21) **Migi chūdan gyaku-zuki**

Step forward with the left foot into a left front stance while delivering a right middle-level reverse punch.

• Step forward with the right foot while extending the left arm out to the left side, leaving the elbow bent slightly. At the same time, pull the right fist back so that the underside of the right wrist is positioned above the left elbow.

22) **Migi chūdan morote-uke**

Step forward with the right foot into a right front stance while performing an inside-to-outside block with the right arm, augmented by the left fist, which presses against the inside of the right elbow. The left fist provides support when blocking to enable a more effective technique.

• Draw the left foot across the rear to the right side, pivoting on the right foot to turn the body 270 degrees to the left (to face toward the right side). At the same time, pull the left fist up to above the right shoulder and thrust the right fist out across the chest and below the left underarm.

23) *Hidari gedan-barai*

Shift into a left front stance facing the right side while performing a left downward block.

• Open the left hand and thrust it upward in front of the body at an angle to the right.

24) *Migi jōdan age-uke*

Step forward with the right foot at a 45-degree angle to the right into a right front stance while performing a right upper-level rising block.

23

24

25

26

• Draw the right foot back, pivoting on the left foot to turn the body 135 degrees to the right while pulling the right fist up to above the left shoulder and thrusting the left fist out across the chest.

25) *Migi gedan-barai*

Shift into a right front stance while performing a right downward block.

• Open the right hand and thrust it upward in front of the body at an angle to the left.

26) *Hidari jōdan age-uke*

Step forward with the left foot at a 45-degree angle to the left into a left front stance while performing a left upper-level rising block with a *kiai* ("*eei!*").

Naore

(*Naore* is a command to return to a natural-posture stance.)

• Draw the left foot back, placing it beside the right foot in an open V stance. At the same time, cross the arms in front of the body with the left arm above the right.

• Extend the arms in front of the body so that the fists are positioned in front of the hips as in the original ready position, and maintain a state of physical and mental readiness (*zanshin*).

Heian Nidan: Technical Analysis

Movements 1–3

1) *Hidari jōdan uchi haiwan-uke*

In response to an upper-level punch from the left side, pull both arms up in a sharp whipping motion, blocking the attack with a left upper-level inside-to-outside back-arm block.

2a) *Migi jōdan tettsui-uchi*

As the opponent delivers a subsequent upper-level punch, deflect the attack with left hand while simultaneously countering with a right upper-level hammer-fist strike to the opponent's elbow.

2b) *Migi chūdan ura-zuki*

When the opponent is at close range, deflect his upper-level punch with the left hand while delivering a right close punch.

3) As the opponent delivers another punch to the midsection, draw the left arm out to the side to block the attack with the left elbow.

4) *Hidari chūdan zuki*

Immediately following the block, straighten the left elbow to counter with a left middle-level punch.

1

2

3

4

Movements 7–8

1) From a left back stance, sidestep a punch from the right side by moving the left foot forward one half-step.

2) *Migi jōdan yoko-keage/Migi jōdan yoko-mawashi uraken-uchi*
   Immediately counter with a simultaneous right upper-level side snap kick and right upper-level side round back-fist strike.

3) *Hidari chūdan shutō-uke*
   In response to a punch from the opposite side, plant the kicking foot on the floor, shifting into a right back stance while deflecting the strike with a left middle-level knife-hand block.

1   2   3

Movement 11

1) In response to an opponent's middle-level punch from the front, perform a pressing block with the left hand while stepping forward with the right foot.

2) *Migi chūdan nukite*
   Shift into a right front stance and counter with a right middle-level spear hand to the opponent's solar plexus.

1   2

Movements 16–18

1) In response to a front snap kick delivered by an opponent positioned at a 45-degree angle to the left, shift the left leg to the left while swinging the right arm downward in a large sweeping motion to block the kick.

2) *Migi chūdan gyaku uchi-uke*

   As the opponent immediately follows through with a punch, perform a right middle-level reverse inside-to-outside block while turning the hips to *gyaku hanmi* (45-degree angle to the front, with the hip on the side opposite to the front leg pushed forward).

3) *Migi chūdan mae-geri*

   Counter with a right middle-level front snap kick.

4) *Hidari chūdan gyaku-zuki*

   Step forward with the right foot into a right front stance while delivering a left middle-level reverse punch, completing the punch as the foot makes contact with the floor.

1

2

3

4

Ura-zuki (Close punch) 裏突き

Ura-zuki, a technique for close-range strikes, can be used for attacks targeting the solar plexus and the side of the body. When delivering *ura-zuki*, the elbow remains bent slightly and the fist rotates only to the point where the back of the fist faces downward when completed.

Practicing Ura-zuki

Stance: *Soto hachiji-dachi* (open V stance) to *zenkutsu-dachi* (front stance)

1) Stand in an open V stance with both fists positioned in front of the hips.
2) Advance the left foot one half-step and extend the left hand out in front of the face to deflect an opponent's upper-level punch. At the same time, draw the right fist up to above the right hip with the back of the fist facing outward.
3) Advance the left foot the remaining half-step into a front stance and rotate the hips so they face the front. At the same time, pull the left hand back to beside the right ear to direct the opponent's punch past the head while thrusting the right fist forward to deliver a close punch. Rotate the right fist 90 degrees as it approaches the target so that the back of the fist faces downward at the moment of impact.
   • Return to the original ready position and repeat the exercise several times.

1

2

3

Jiyū ippon kumite (Free-style one-step kumite) 自由一本組手

Practicing *jiyū ippon kumite* enables students to learn the effective use of *maai* (distance between opponents when sparring) when launching an attack, as well as proper breathing during sparring. Additionally, *jiyū ippon kumite* training provides students with the opportunity to learn how to block and counterattack under free-style sparring conditions.

Proper etiquette when practicing *jiyū ippon kumite*

1) Both opponents face each other standing in closed V stances.
2) Both opponents exchange bows. (Bows are also exchanged at the end of each *jiyū ippon kumite* session.)
3) Both opponents assume open V stances.
4) Both opponents assume free-sparring stances. Beginning students should stand in a slightly shortened front stance with the front arm (the arm on the same side of the body as the front leg) bent slightly and positioned out in front of the body. The front fist is aimed at the opponent's face. The back arm should be tucked against the solar plexus with the fist pointing in the general direction of the opponent's midsection.

When practicing *jiyū ippon kumite*, the attacker tries to close the distance between himself and his opponent (*maai*) while looking for an opportunity to launch an attack. The defender may strategically move so as to try to prevent the attacker from closing within easy striking distance, but must not simply run away from the attacker's approaches. Also, after delivering the counterattack, the defender should immediately remove himself from the attacker's striking distance while maintaining a state of physical and mental readiness (*zanshin*).

1

2

3

4

Jōdan-zuki (Upper-level punch) 1

Block: *Jōdan nagashi-uke* (Upper-level sweeping block) / ***Counterattack***: *Chūdan ura-zuki* (Middle-level close punch)

1) The attacker (right) and defender face off in free-sparring stances.
2) The attacker steps forward and delivers a right upper-level lunge punch. / As the attacker initiates the attack, the defender immediately steps forward with the front foot to meet the attacker's strike, blocking with a left upper-level sweeping block.
3) The defender guides the attacker's punch past the side of his head while simultaneously countering with a right middle-level close punch.
4) The defender immediately pushes the attacker away with the blocking hand while shifting the back foot to the rear and left at a 45-degree angle, maintaining a state of physical and mental readiness (*zanshin*).

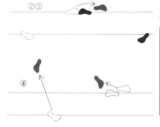

Points to remember

1) Timing is critical when stepping forward to execute a sweeping block; even a slight error in timing could result in a failed block. Accordingly, this technique should first be practiced slowly until it can be performed with confidence.
2) The close punch must be delivered as the attacker is still moving forward, utilizing his momentum to ensure an effective counterattack.

1

2

3

4

Jōdan-zuki 2

Block: *Jōdan age-uke* (Upper-level rising block) / ***Counterattack***: *Chūdan kizami mawashi-geri* (Middle-level short roundhouse kick), *Chūdan gyaku-zuki* (Middle-level reverse punch)

1) The attacker (right) and defender face off in free-sparring stances.

2) The attacker steps forward and delivers a right upper-level lunge punch. / Pivoting on the rear foot, the defender draws the front foot back at a 45-degree angle to the left, shifting into a right front stance while blocking with a right upper-level rising block.

3) The defender opens his right hand to suppress the attacker's punching arm while raising the front leg in preparation to launch a counterattack.

4) The defender delivers a right middle-level roundhouse kick to the attacker's solar plexus.

5) The defender plants the kicking foot forward into a right front stance while following through with a left middle-level reverse punch.

6) The defender immediately deflects the attacker's punching arm with the right hand while drawing the front foot back, maintaining a state of physical and mental readiness (*zanshin*).

1

2

Points to remember

1) Setting the right hand on the attacker's punching arm after blocking enables the defender to maintain balance when kicking and, by grabbing and pulling the attacker's arm, also serves to throw the attacker off-balance.

2) The reverse punch should be delivered at the same instant that the foot touches the floor after the kick.

3

4   5   6

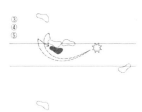

Jōdan-zuki 3

Block: *Osae-uke* (Pressing block) / **Counterattack**: *Chūdan tobi mae-geri* (Middle-level jumping front kick), *Jōdan yoko-mawashi uraken-uchi* (Upper-level side round back-fist strike)

1) The attacker (right) and defender face off in free-sparring stances.
2) The attacker steps forward and delivers a right upper-level lunge punch. / Using the front hand, the defender forces down the attacker's punching arm with a pressing block. Utilizing the reaction from the block, the defender simultaneously leaps into the air and rotates the hips to the left while delivering a right jumping front kick to the attacker's midsection, immediately followed by a right side round back-fist strike to the face.
3) The defender lands on the ground with the right leg forward, maintaining a state of physical and mental readiness (*zanshin*).

Points to remember

The rotation of the body in mid-air is a form of evasive body-shifting (*tai-sabaki*).

1   2   3

Chūdan-zuki (Middle-level punch) 1

Block: *Chūdan soto ude-uke* (Middle-level outside-to-inside block) / ***Counterattack***:
Chūdan gyaku-zuki (Middle-level reverse punch)

1) The attacker (right) and defender face off in free-sparring stances.
2) The attacker steps forward and delivers a right middle-level lunge punch. / Pivoting on the front foot, the defender shifts the rear leg 45 degrees to the left into a left front stance while blocking with a left middle-level outside-to-inside block.
3) The defender counters with a right middle-level reverse punch.
4) The defender immediately deflects the attacker's punching arm with the left hand while drawing the front foot back, maintaining a state of physical and mental readiness (*zanshin*).

Points to remember

1) Shifting the rear leg when blocking serves to shift the body (*tai-sabaki*) out of the path of the attack.
2) The reverse-punch counterattack must be fully executed before pulling away from the attacker.

1

2

3

4

Chūdan-zuki 2

Block: *Gedan-barai* (Downward block) / ***Counterattack***: *Chūdan yoko-geri kekomi* (Middle-level side thrust kick), *Jōdan yoko-mawashi uraken-uchi* (Upper-level side round back-fist strike)

1) The attacker (right) and defender face off in free-sparring stances.
2) The attacker steps forward and delivers a right middle-level lunge punch. / Pivoting on the rear foot, the defender draws the front foot back at a 45-degree angle to the left, shifting into a right front stance while blocking with a right downward block.
3) The defender delivers a right middle-level side thrust kick with the front leg.
4) The defender steps forward with the kicking leg into a right front stance, planting the foot on the far side of the attacker's front leg. At the same time the defender follows through with an upper-level side round back-fist strike.
5) While retracting the right fist following the back-fist strike, the defender pivots on the front foot to face the attacker and moves out of the attacker's striking distance, maintaining a state of physical and mental readiness (*zanshin*).

Points to remember

1) When executing the side thrust kick with the front leg, do not allow the upper body to lean too far in the direction opposite to the target.
2) Utilize the forward momentum of the body following the kick to deliver a powerful back-fist strike.

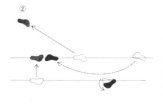

1

2

3

4

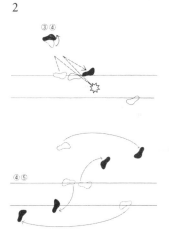

5

Chūdan-zuki 3

Block: *Gyaku gedan seiryūtō-uke* (Reverse lower-level ox-jaw block) / **Counterattack**: *Jōdan yoko-mawashi uraken-uchi* (Upper-level side round back-fist strike)

1) The attacker (right) and defender face off in free-sparring stances.

2) The attacker steps forward and delivers a right middle-level lunge punch. / The defender steps straight back with the left leg into a right front stance while blocking with a left reverse lower-level ox-jaw block. At the same time, the defender draws the right hand, formed into a fist, back to above the left shoulder with the back of the fist facing outward.

3) The defender, driving off the rear foot, slides the front foot forward (*yori-ashi*) while countering with a right upper-level side round back-fist strike.

4) The defender draws the front foot back one half-step while retracting the right fist following the back-fist strike, maintaining a state of physical and mental readiness (*zanshin*).

1   2

3   4

Points to remember

1) Although the defender simultaneously prepares for the back-fist-strike counterattack while blocking, it is important to realize that the block is of primary importance. If the defender cannot sufficiently block the attacker's strike, he may not have an opportunity to launch a counterattack.

2) Thrust off the back foot to generate forward momentum when delivering the back-fist strike.

Mae-geri (Front snap kick) 1

Block: *Gedan-barai* (Downward block) / **Counterattack**: *Chūdan gyaku-zuki* (Middle-level reverse punch)

1) The attacker (right) and defender face off in free-sparring stances.

2) The attacker steps forward and delivers a right middle-level front snap kick. / Pivoting on the front foot, the defender shifts the rear leg 45 degrees to the right into a left front stance while blocking with a left downward block.

3) The defender immediately counters with a right middle-level reverse punch.

4) The defender pulls the striking hand back while drawing the front foot away from the attacker, simultaneously extending the left arm to keep the attacker in check and maintaining a state of physical and mental readiness (*zanshin*).

Mae-geri 2

Block: *Gedan seiken jūji-uke* (Lower-level fist X-block) / **Counterattack**: *Jōdan uchi-mawashi shutō-uchi* (Upper-level inside round knife-hand strike)

1) The attacker (right) and defender face off in free-sparring stances.
2) The attacker steps forward and delivers a right middle-level front snap kick. / The instant that the attacker begins to deliver the kick, the defender lunges forward off the rear leg into an elongated left front stance and blocks with a lower-level fist X-block, with the left fist above the right fist.

   Utilizing the impact of the kick, the defender sweeps the attacker's leg past using the right arm while shifting the back foot to the left at a 45-degree angle, simultaneously drawing the left hand back in preparation to deliver a knife-hand strike.
3) Utilizing the rotation of the body (*tenshin*), the defender counters with a left upper-level inside round knife-hand strike.
4) The defender pulls the striking hand back while drawing the front foot away from the attacker, maintaining a state of physical and mental readiness (*zanshin*).

Yoko-geri kekomi (Side thrust kick) 1

Block: *Chūdan haiwan-uke* (Middle-level back-arm block) / **Counterattack**: *Jōdan ushiro-mawashi empi-uchi* (Upper-level back round elbow strike)

1) The attacker (right) and defender face off in free-sparring stances.
2) The attacker steps forward and delivers a right middle-level side thrust kick. / The defender, pivoting on the front foot, shifts the back foot to the left while blocking with a left middle-level back-arm block.
3) Following through with the motion initiated by the block, the defender draws the front foot back one half-step and, pivoting on the same foot, rotates the body 180 degrees to the right, shifting into a right front stance behind the attacker while delivering a right upper-level back round elbow strike.
4) Pivoting on the same foot, the defender turns the body 180 degrees in the opposite direction to once again face the attacker while maintaining a state of physical and mental readiness (*zanshin*).

Yoko-geri kekomi 2

Block: *Chūdan soto ude-uke* (Middle-level outside-to-inside block) / ***Counterattack***:
Chūdan gyaku-zuki (Middle-level reverse punch)

1) The attacker (right) and defender face off in free-sparring stances.
2) The attacker steps forward and delivers a right middle-level side thrust kick. / Pivoting on the front foot, the defender shifts the rear leg 45 degrees to the left into a left front stance while blocking with a left middle-level outside-to-inside block.
3) The defender counters with a right middle-level reverse punch.
4) The defender pulls the punching hand back while drawing the front foot away from the attacker, simultaneously extending the left arm to keep the attacker in check and maintaining a state of physical and mental readiness (*zanshin*).

1

2

3

4

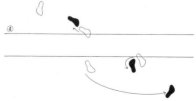

Yoko-geri kekomi 3

Block: *Chūdan awase seiryūtō-uke* (Middle-level two-handed ox-jaw block) / ***Counterattack***: *Jōdan tate-zuki* (Upper-level vertical-fist punch)

1) The attacker (right) and defender face off in free-sparring stances.
2) The attacker steps forward and delivers a right middle-level side thrust kick. / The defender, pivoting on the rear foot, draws the front foot back and to the right at a 45-degree angle into a right front stance while blocking with a middle-level two-handed ox-jaw block.
3) The defender, driving off the rear foot, counters with a right upper-level vertical-fist punch.
4) The defender pulls the striking hand back while drawing the front foot away from the attacker, maintaining a state of physical and mental readiness (*zanshin*).

1

2

3

4

Mawashi-geri (Roundhouse kick) 1

Block: *Jōdan haiwan-uke* (Upper-level back-arm block) / ***Counterattack***: *Chūdan gyaku-zuki* (Middle-level reverse punch)

1) The attacker (right) and defender face off in free-sparring stances.
2) The attacker steps forward and delivers a right upper-level roundhouse kick. / The defender, pivoting on the front foot, draws the rear foot out to the right side, turning 45 degrees to the left into a left front stance while blocking with a left upper-level back-arm block.
3) The defender counters with a right middle-level reverse punch.
4) The defender pulls the striking hand back while drawing the front foot away from the attacker, maintaining a state of physical and mental readiness (*zanshin*).

1

2

3

4

Ushiro-geri (Back kick) 1

Block: *Chūdan sukui-uke* (Middle-level scooping block) / **Counterattack**: *Ashi-barai* (Leg sweep), *Gedan gyaku-zuki* (Downward reverse punch)

1) The attacker (right) and defender face off in free-sparring stances.
2) The attacker steps forward and delivers a right middle-level back kick. / The instant that the attacker initiates his attack, the defender lunges forward to evade the kick, moving behind the attacker with the front foot positioned alongside the attacker's supporting foot while blocking with a right middle-level scooping block.
3–4) With the blocking hand under the attacker's kicking leg, the defender sweeps the supporting leg, lifting and dropping the attacker to the floor.

1

2

3

4

5) The defender immediately counters with a right downward reverse punch.

5

6) The defender pulls the striking hand back and maintains a state of physical and mental readiness (*zanshin*).

6

CHAPTER **5**

From Self-Defense to Nunchaku

LESSON 13

- Lessons 10–12: Review (Approx. 40 min.)
- Nidan-geri (Double jump kick)
- Tobi yoko-geri (Jumping side kick)

Nidan-geri (Double jump kick) 二段蹴り

Nidan-geri, a type of *tobi-geri* (jumping kick), comprises two successive front snap kicks performed while leaping in the air.

Practicing nidan-geri 1

Stance: *Heisoku-dachi* (closed parallel stance)

1) Assume a closed parallel stance with the arms extended downward to the sides.
2) Lift the right knee, drawing the right foot alongside the left knee.
3) Deliver a right upper-level front snap kick.
4) Spring off the left leg immediately after the right leg has reached full extension and deliver a left upper-level front snap kick while retracting the right leg.
5) Pull the left leg back following the second kick as the right foot lands on the floor.
   - Return to the original ready position from step 1 and repeat the exercise several times, alternating sides.

1

2   3   4   5

Practicing nidan-geri 2

Stance: *Zenkutsu-dachi* (front stance) to *zenkutsu-dachi*

• Assume a left front stance with the arms extended downward to the sides.

1) Spring off the left foot and deliver a right middle-level front snap kick using a snapping motion of the knee. At the same time, draw the left leg up under the body.

2) Deliver a left upper-level front snap kick while pulling back the right leg.

• Pull the left leg back after the second kick as the right foot lands on the floor, then step forward with the left foot into a left front stance.

Points to remember

1) Because the second kick must be completed at the height of the jump, it is necessary to leap high into the air.

2) Tighten the stomach muscles when performing *nidan-geri* to ensure that the upper body does not lean backwards when kicking.

1

2

Tobi yoko-geri (Jumping side kick) 飛横蹴り

Tobi yoko-geri, or *kesa-geri*, is another type of *tobi-geri* (jumping kick), consisting of a side kick delivered while leaping in the air.

Practicing tobi yoko-geri

Stance: *Heisoku-dachi* (closed parallel stance)

• Assume a closed parallel stance with the head turned facing the left and the arms extended downward to the sides.

1) Lift the left knee up toward the chest while springing off the right leg.
2) Direct the edge of the left foot (*sokutō*) toward the target.
3) Sharply extend the left knee and drive the heel of the left foot to the side and downward at an angle to deliver the kick. At the same time, draw the right foot upward toward the inner thigh. The motion of the right leg enables the delivery of a more powerful kick while also serving to protect the groin.
   • Land on the right foot and retract the left leg, returning to the same position as step 1.
   • Place the left foot on the floor and return to the original closed parallel stance.

Points to remember

1) Complete the kick at the height of the jump.
2) An unstable landing after the kick may leave you vulnerable to a counterattack. Accordingly, in addition to practicing the kick, it is necessary to practice landing properly.

1   2   3

Practical application of tobi yoko-geri

1) Step out to the right side to elude an opponent's middle-level lunge-punch attack.
2) Upon planting the right foot, draw the left knee up sharply.
3) Leap up off the right leg and kick with the left leg to the side of the opponent's head.
4) Land behind the opponent at an approximately 45-degree angle, planting the right foot on the floor first.

Points to remember

1) Wait until the instant before the attacker completes the delivery of his punch to shift the body (*tai-sabaki*) out of the path of the attack.
2) Take into account the distance between yourself and your opponent (*maai*) prior to leaping to ensure the delivery of an effective *tobi yoko-geri*.

1

2

3

4

LESSON 14

- Lesson 13: Review (Approx. 30 min.)
- Jiyū kumite (Free sparring)
- Self-defense techniques
- Using training equipment

Jiyū kumite (Free sparring) 自由組手

Unlike *yakusoku kumite* (promise sparring), introduced earlier, in *jiyū kumite* neither technique or target is predetermined—any type of attack may be used to strike any target. This type of *kumite* enables participants to fully employ their strength, spirit and abilities while exchanging a variety of offensive and defensive techniques. It is essential, however, that each punch, strike, and kick be controlled, stopping a single *sun* (about 3 cm, or $1^1/_4$ inches) before making contact with the intended target (a practice called *sun-dome*, meaning "to stop one *sun* [before contact]").

While *sun-dome* is an indispensable component of *jiyū kumite*, the aim is not to relax just prior to making contact, but rather to deliver strikes with force and spirit so that their explosive power culminates directly in front of the target.

1

2   3

1) Opponent A (left) delivers a left jab as opponent B leans back to move out of striking distance.

2) B immediately drives forward with a right reverse punch as A steps out at an angle with the front leg, blocking the punch with a right reverse downward block.

3) A responds with a left front snap kick, which B blocks using a right downward block while stepping back at an angle with the front leg.

4) B counters with a left reverse punch, catching A in the midsection.

5) B draws the front leg back and steps forward with the opposite leg, following through with a right reverse punch. A steps out of the path of the attack, raising the right leg in preparation for a counterattack.

6) A delivers a right upper-level side thrust kick.

4

5

6

Self defense techniques 護身術

The ultimate objective of self defense is to be able to protect oneself in the face of any threat, regardless of when or where it may occur or what form it may take. While it goes without saying that technical skills are essential in achieving this goal, ideally self defense also includes being able to confront an adversary without fear, as well as the ability to concentrate sufficient energy in the lower abdomen (*tanden* in Japanese) in order to execute movements as circumstances demand, focusing the energy effectively to deliver techniques with explosive power.

Regular comprehensive training in karate's fundamental components—basics (*kihon*), *kata*, sparring (*kumite*), proper breathing, stretching, weapons training, and meditation—enables the development of these essential abilities and the cultivating of energy. And being able to call on these skills at any time represents the highest form of self defense.

Broadly speaking, self defense means protecting oneself from all forms of danger, including sickness, accidents, pollution, and natural disasters. Enhancing the natural healing powers that all humans are born with while maximizing life force makes possible not only the ability to protect oneself from harm but also shows us how to apply ourselves and interact with others within a social framework.

The section that follows presents only the technical aspects of dealing with a variety of self-defense situations.

Scenario 1: Grabbed from behind

1) This scenario assumes that an assailant has approached from behind, locked his arm around your neck and taken hold of your left wrist.
2) Open the left hand while rotating the wrist in the direction of the thumb to break free from the assailant's grasp. At the same time, step forward with left foot at an angle to the left into a narrow left front stance while delivering a right back elbow strike to the midsection.
3) As the assailant recoils, rotate the hips in the opposite direction and deliver a left upper-level back round elbow strike.

1   2

2 (opposite-side view)

3

Scenario 2: Grabbed from behind

1) This scenario assumes that an assailant has approached from behind and wrapped his arms around your upper body.

2) Draw the heel of the left foot up in a swift motion toward the buttocks to kick the assailant in the groin.

3) If the assailant does not relinquish his hold, drive both hands straight out in front of the body while stepping forward with the right foot into a right front stance.

4) As soon as the assailant's grip has been broken, turn around to the left, shifting into a left front stance while delivering a left side-elbow strike to the midsection.

1

2

3

4

Scenario 3: Held from the front

1) In this scenario, an assailant has suddenly grabbed both of your wrists.
2) Deliver a right front snap kick to the assailant's groin.
3) Step forward with the right foot to the left of the assailant, grab his right wrist with the right hand and raise it directly upward to break his grip.
4) Twist the assailant's arm and draw it downward. Keep him restrained by pressing down on the back of his right elbow while delivering a kick to the face with the heel of the left foot.

1

2

3

4

Scenario 4: Confronting two assailants

1) This scenario assumes that two assailants have approached and each has taken hold of one wrist.
2) Draw the right foot up and over the left arm of the assailant on the right-hand side.
3) Deliver a right side thrust kick to the midsection of the assailant on the right.
4) Pull the right foot back and immediately deliver a right front snap kick to the midsection of the assailant on the left-hand side.

1

2

3

4

Scenario 5: Confronting three assailants

1) In this scenario, two assailants have grabbed your wrists and shoulders while a third assailant approaches from the front. Deliver a right front snap kick to the midsection of the assailant in front.

2) Retract the right foot and drive it back to deliver a right back kick to the midsection of the assailant located behind and to the right.

3) Turn to the right and plant the right foot on the floor to the right of the third assailant, shifting into a straddle-leg stance while delivering a right side-elbow strike to the midsection.

1

2

3

Using training equipment

Training equipment commonly used for karate includes a punching board (*maki-wara*), punching bag, wooden sword (*bokutō*) for swinging, and dumbbells. In this section, only the *makiwara* and punching bag will be covered.

Training with a makiwara

The *makiwara*, which can be used to practice punching, striking, and kicking, offers more than merely a means of strengthening the hands and feet. By training with a *makiwara*, karate students can learn which muscles to tighten at the moment of impact, how to effectively use the hips, and how to optimize stances to ensure stability and balance.

A substitute for a *makiwara* can be fashioned out of thick foam padding or a portion of a tire affixed to a solid wall or panel.

1) *Yoko-mawashi uraken-uchi* (**side round back-fist strike**)
   Practice performing back-fist strikes while standing in a straddle-leg stance. Keep the wrist firmly locked and rotate the fist outward at the moment of impact.
2) *Chūdan gyaku-zuki* (**middle-level reverse punch**)
   Stand in a front stance and deliver reverse punches with the feeling of punching from the lower abdomen. Keep the elbow of the punching arm inside against the body and sharply thrust off the rear foot to launch each punch.

1 2

Training with a punching bag

A punching bag can be used to practice punching, striking, and kicking techniques. By swinging the bag in different directions, students can practice accurately tracking and striking a moving target. As a result, they can learn proper distancing (*maai*) when attacking while developing lower body strength capable of withstanding the rebound that results when delivering blows to a heavy target.

When practicing kicking techniques, the supporting leg and, in the case of jumping kicks, the leg used to leap into the air are of particular importance. So, too, is the pulling back of the kicking leg immediately after the kick has been delivered. Lead with the hips when kicking and fully utilize the strength of the lower abdomen.

The following photos show how a punching bag can be used to practice various kicking techniques.

1) *Mae-geri* (front snap kick)
2) *Ushiro-geri* (back kick)
3) *Yoko-kekomi* (side thrust kick)
4) *Mawashi-geri* (roundhouse kick)

1

2

3

4

5) *Gyaku mikazuki-geri* (reverse crescent kick)
6) *Ushiro mawashi-geri* (back roundhouse kick)
7) *Tobi mae-geri* (jumping front kick)
8) *Tobi yoko-geri* (jumping side kick)
9) *Tobi mawashi-geri* (jumping roundhouse kick)

5

6

7

8

9

LESSON 15

- **Lesson 14: Review (Approx. 30 min.)**
- **Introduction to nunchaku**
- **Tameshi-wari (Test breaking)**

Nunchaku ヌンチャク

The *nunchaku*, made from two hardwood sticks connected by a rope or chain, represents one of the traditional fighting arts, or *kobudō*. The *nunchaku*, with a history dating back to the early 1600s, was first adapted from common work tools in Okinawa during a period when the use of conventional weapons was prohibited, providing ordinary citizens with a means of protecting themselves and their property. Accordingly, it shares a sibling relationship with karate, which spread from China to Okinawa and also developed rapidly under a policy that prohibited the use of weapons.

While training with the *nunchaku* helps to sharpen reflexes and develop wrist and elbow strength, the weapon poses a potential risk to beginning students. As such, only a basic introduction will be provided in this section.

1) Jōdan yama-gamae (Upper-level mountain position) 上段山構え
The *nunchaku* is held out in front of the body by the ends of the handles and the rope portion is used for blocking upper-level attacks. After blocking, the handles can be crossed to entangle an opponent's weapon.

2) Chūdan yama-gamae (Middle-level mountain position) 中段山構え
This technique is similar to *jōdan yama-gamae* except that the hands are positioned in front of the hips. The rope of the *nunchaku* is used to block middle-level attacks and the handles can be crossed immediately after blocking to grab hold of an opponent's weapon.

1

2

3) **Gyaku shihō-uke (Reverse square block)** 逆四方受け

Hold the *nunchaku* at the ends of the handles and cross the arms in front of the chest so that the *nunchaku* and arms describe a square around the face. This technique enables upper-level strikes from above or the side to be blocked, followed by an attack using either hand to swing the *nunchaku.*

3

4) **Sokumen jōdan gamae (Upper flank position)** 側面上段構え

Holding the end of one of the handles in the right hand, swing the *nunchaku* up in front of the right side of the body and over the right shoulder, catching the opposite handle below the right underarm with the left hand. This position offers protection for the side of the body while also serving as a ready position from which an attack can be delivered to an opponent's head by swinging the *nunchaku* downward with a snap of the right wrist.

5) **Jōdan suihei gamae (Upper-level horizontal position)** 上段水平構え

Grasping the ends of the handles, extend both arms upward and forward at an angle while tautly holding the *nunchaku* in a horizontal position. This posture, also called *ichimonji gamae,* is a defensive stance against upper-level attacks.

6) **Migi seigan no kamae (Right engagement position)** 右正眼の構え

Seigan no kamae, a ready stance used when facing an opponent, enables almost any type of response to an opponent's actions. Holding the *nunchaku* in the right hand by the ends of both handles, bring the right foot forward into an L stance (*renoji-dachi*) and extend the right arm out in front of the solar plexus, pointing the opposite ends of the handles at the opponent's face.

4

7) **Musubi-gamae (Entangled position)** 結び構え

Holding one of the handles in the right hand, swing the *nunchaku* over the left shoulder and across the back, catching the other handle with the left hand below the right underarm. This position is used as a defensive stance to protect the back as well as a ready position for launching an attack.

8) **Gedan jūji-uke (Lower-level X-block)** 下段十字受け

Thrust both hands downward and cross the handles to block lower-level attacks.

9) **Migi jōdan age-uke (Right upper-level rising block)** 右上段揚受け

Holding the ends of the handles in the right hand, draw the *nunchaku* upward to block upper-level attacks.

5

10) **Migi jōdan gyaku age-uke** 右上段逆揚受け
　　(Right upper-level reverse rising block)

This block is similar to *migi jōdan age-uke* except that the right hand is positioned on the left-hand side of the body, with the back of the right hand facing forward.

6

7   8   9   10

11) Dai-jōdan gamae—Shajō-gaeshi　大上段構え斜状返し
(Upper open position—Diagonal strike)

In *dai-jōdan gamae*, the *nunchaku* is positioned vertically down the back with one hand holding the end of one handle above the shoulder on the same side of the body, and the other hand holding the opposite handle at the base of the spine, with the back of the hand resting against the lower back.

Shajō-gaeshi is a striking technique in which the *nunchaku* travels along a downward diagonal course around the body and can be used for strikes targeting the side of the body, the carotid artery, the torso, the knee or, should the opponent be holding a weapon, the wrist. This technique also serves to discourage attacks from the rear.

When performing *shajō-gaeshi*, draw the opposite hand up and out in front of the body to keep it out of the path of the *nunchaku*. Once the free handle has completed

1 (rear view)   2 (side view)

its course around the body, immediately bring the striking hand up to its original starting position above the shoulder, swinging the *nunchaku* back along the course it traveled. Return the opposite hand to behind the back to catch the *nunchaku* and return to *dai-jōdan gamae*.

By modifying the movement, *shajō-gaeshi* can be transformed into *tsubame-gaeshi* (swallow strike), as demonstrated on the following page.

1   2   3   4

12) **Tsubame-gaeshi (Swallow strike)** 燕返し

Starting from *dai-jōdan gamae*, use the hand positioned behind the back to swing the *nunchaku* from below out in front of the body and upward in a circular path while lifting the leg on the same side. As the *nunchaku* circles around, swing it across the front of the body as in *shajō-gaeshi*.

1 2 3 4

13) **Fūsha-gaeshi (Windmill strike)** 風車返し

From *sokumen jōdan gamae*, use the upper hand to swing the *nunchaku* over the shoulder and down alongside the body, and then immediately back up to the original starting position.

1 2 3

14) Omote-sempūrin (Front whirlwind)　表旋風輪

From *sokumen jōdan gamae*, use the lower hand to swing the *nunchaku* up and over the shoulder on the same side. The free hand travels across the front of the body to grasp the handle on the far side of the body to assume a *sokumen jōdan gamae* on the opposite side.

1　　　2　　　3　　　4

15) Ura-sempūrin (Rear whirlwind)　裏旋風輪

From *dai-jōdan gamae*, draw the *nunchaku* out with the hand behind the back and swing it over the shoulder on the same side. Reach behind the back with the free hand and catch the handle to assume a *dai-jōdan gamae* on the opposite side.

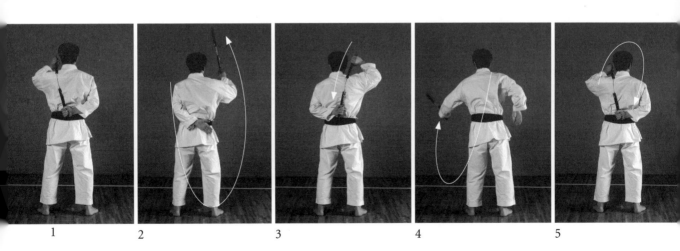

1　　　2　　　3　　　4　　　5

16) Gyaku shajō-gaeshi (Reverse diagonal strike) 逆斜上返し

From *musubi-gamae*, use the hand positioned above the shoulder to swing the *nunchaku* downward at an angle around the body and out to the side. Immediately swing the *nunchaku* back along the course it traveled, bringing the striking hand to its original position and returning to *musubi-gamae*.

1   2   3   4

17) Happū-gaeshi (Figure-eight strike) 八風返し

Beginning from *dai-jōdan gamae*, use the hand positioned above the shoulder to swing the *nunchaku* downward at an angle across the front of the body, then upward and back across the front of the body to describe a horizontal figure-eight pattern. After completing a single figure eight, perform *shajō-gaeshi* and return to the initial *dai-jōdan gamae* position.

1   2   3   4   5   6

18) **Komata-gaeshi (Inner-thigh reversal)**　小俣返し

Komata-gaeshi provides a means of initiating a change in direction to launch a new technique. The following photos show a sequence of moves that begin with *dai-jōdan gamae* and *happū-gaeshi*, followed by a change of direction using *komata-gaeshi*.

1 2 3 4

5 6 7 8

A precision strike shatters an apple tossed into the air.

In this photo, the author demonstrates a *nunchaku* technique in response to a theoretical attack. The author has eluded the attack while leaping into the air and simultaneously launches a spinning counterattack.

Tameshi-wari (Test breaking) 試し割り

Tameshi-wari—testing the effectiveness of a technique by attempting to break boards, tiles or other objects—does not represent the true meaning of karate. But, as it is a general rule of karate that all kicks, punches, and strikes must be brought to a halt just before making contact with their intended targets, *tameshi-wari* provides an opportunity to confirm the actual power of various offensive techniques. A similar practice also exists in kendō (Japanese fencing), called *tameshi-giri* (test cutting).

Accordingly, breaking boards is not an activity that should be practiced exclusively; it is something that can be accomplished naturally upon mastering the basic techniques of karate through regular and diligent training.

The most important factors in successful *tameshi-wari* are speed, timing, and focus at the moment of impact.

The following photographs show some examples of *tameshi-wari*.

A board tossed into the air is split with a back-first strike.

1

2

3

An apple placed on top of an assistant's head is shattered with a back roundhouse kick.

Shihō-wari (Board breaking in four directions) 四方割り

Shihō-wari, in which multiple boards held in different surrounding positions are broken one after the other, represents an advanced form of *tameshi-wari*. When performing *shihō-wari*, the practitioner must move smoothly from one location to the next, delivering successive strikes in each direction with sufficient speed, strength and focus to break each board with a single blow.

The following photographs show board breaking in four directions using a combination of arm and leg techniques.

1) The author addresses the first of four boards prior to delivering the first strike.
2) He delivers a reverse punch to break the first board.
3) An elbow strike in the opposite direction splits the second board.
4) A front snap kick is used to break the third board.
5) And a downward knife-hand strike breaks the fourth and final board.

1

2

3

4

5

CHAPTER 6

Building Future Training Menus

Lessons 16 through 18 comprise a variety of example training menus based on techniques and exercises introduced in earlier chapters. The following menus are only examples of possible training programs; actual lesson menus should be prepared with the aim of encouraging continued training, taking into careful consideration such factors as age and physical health.

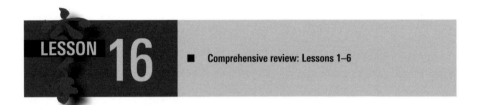

LESSON 16

■ Comprehensive review: Lessons 1–6

Lesson menu example

1) Warm-up exercises (10 min.)
2) *Kihon* (basic) training (50 min.)

a. In place

- From *soto hachiji-dachi* (open V stance)
  Sonoba-zuki (punching while standing in place)
  Uraken-uchi (back-fist strike)
  Jōdan age-uke (upper-level rising block)
  Chūdan soto ude-uke (middle-level outside-to-inside block)
  Chūdan uchi ude-uke (middle-level inside-to-outside block)

- From *heisoku-dachi* (closed parallel stance)
  Mae-geri (front snap kick)
  Yoko-geri ke-age (side snap kick)
  Yoko-geri kekomi (side thrust kick)

- From *zenkutsu-dachi* (front stance)
  Gyaku-zuki (reverse punch)
  Empi-uchi (elbow strike)
  Mae-geri (front snap kick)

- From *kōkutsu-dachi* (back stance)
  Chūdan shutō-uke (middle-level knife-hand block)

b. Stepping

- From *zenkutsu-dachi* (front stance)
  Oi-zuki (lunge punch)
  Jōdan age-uke (upper-level rising block)
  Chūdan soto ude-uke (middle-level outside-to-inside block)
  Chūdan uchi ude-uke (middle-level inside-to-outside block)
  Mae-geri (front snap kick)

- From *kiba-dachi* (straddle-leg stance)
  Yoko-geri ke-age (side snap kick)
  Yoko-geri kekomi (side thrust kick)

- From *kōkutsu-dachi* (back stance)
  Chūdan shutō-uke (middle-level knife-hand block)

3) *Kumite*: *Gohon kumite* (Five-step *kumite*) (20 min.)

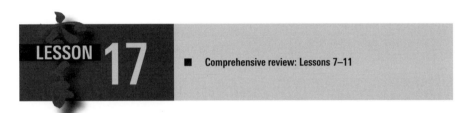

LESSON 17 ■ Comprehensive review: Lessons 7–11

Lesson menu example

1) Warm-up exercises (10 min.)
2) *Kihon* (basic) training (30 min.)

a. In place
  - From *zenkutsu-dachi* (front stance)
    Gyaku-zuki (reverse punch)
    Shutō-uchi (knife-hand strike)
    Mae-geri (front snap kick)
    Mawashi-geri (roundhouse kick)

  - From *kiba-dachi* (straddle-leg stance)
    Tettsui-uchi (hammer-fist strike)
    Mikazuki-geri (Crescent kick)

  - From *heisoku-dachi* (closed parallel stance)
    Ushiro-geri (back kick)

b. Stepping
  - *Kihon* (basic) combinations: Arm/Leg combinations
  - From *zenkutsu-dachi* (front stance)
    Ushiro-geri (back kick)

3) *Kumite*: *Kihon ippon kumite* (Basic one-step *kumite*) (20 min.)

4) *Kata*: Heian Shodan, Heian Nidan (20 min.)

LESSON 18

- Comprehensive review: Lessons 12–15
- Kata: Tekki Shodan

Lesson menu example

1) Warm-up exercises (10 min.)
2) *Kihon* (basic) training (20 min.)

a. In place
- From *heisoku-dachi* (closed parallel stance)
  Mae-geri (front snap kick)
  Nidan-geri (double jump kick)
  Tobi yoko-geri (jumping side kick)

b. Stepping
- *Kihon* (basic) combinations

3) *Kumite*: *Jiyū ippon kumite* (Free-style one-step *kumite*) (20 min.)
4) Self-defense techniques (10 min.)
5) *Kata*: Tekki Shodan (30 min.)

Kata: Tekki Shodan 鉄騎初段

Kata training commonly begins with the five Heian *kata*, introduced in ascending order starting with Heian Shodan (Heian Number One). Only after Heian Godan (Heian Number Five) has been learned are students taught Tekki Shodan. Since only the first two Heian *kata* have been presented thus far, convention dictates that Heian Sandan (Heian Number Three) be taught next.

Here, however, we will break with tradition and introduce Tekki Shodan, as the practice of this *kata* offers a range of physical therapeutic benefits, particularly for the spine. Students practicing karate as a means of staying in shape are strongly encouraged to include the performance of this *kata* in every training session.

Tekki Shodan, consisting of 27 movements in all, is performed while moving laterally in *kiba-dachi* (straddle-leg stance). Accordingly, the *embusen* (performance line) in Tekki Shodan is a straight horizontal line. Techniques included in the *kata* are back-hand blocks, elbow strikes, downward blocks, hook punches, inside-to-outside blocks, back-fist strikes, outside-to-inside blocks, return-wave kicks, and double-fist punches.

If practiced diligently, Tekki Shodan provides students with an opportunity to master *kiba-dachi*, as the stance is featured almost exclusively throughout the *kata*.

Other areas that require special attention to perform properly include the elbow-strike/downward-block/hook-punch combination, and the distinctive *nami-gaeshi*, or returning wave kick.

Practicing kata: Tekki Shodan

Ready position (***yōi***): From *soto hachiji-dachi* (open V stance) slide the right foot inward, shifting to *heisoku-dachi* (closed parallel stance), and draw the hands toward each other, placing the left hand over the right hand while extending both arms downward at an angle in front of the body with the elbows bent slightly.

1) Turn the head to the right and sharply lower the hips, transferring the body's weight to the right leg. Move the left foot in front of the right leg, placing it on the far side of the right foot to assume a cross-legged stance (*kōsa-dachi*). The arms and hands do not move from the ready position.

   • Transfer the body's weight fully to the left leg and swing the right leg up high in front of the body while crossing the arms in a large motion in front of the chest with the left arm above the right arm.

2) ***Migi fumikomi/Migi chūdan haishu-uke***

   Deliver a right stamping kick to the right side, shifting into a straddle-leg stance while performing a right middle-level back-hand block with a snapping motion of the elbow.

ready (*yōi*)

1

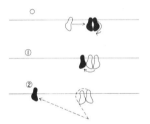

2

3   4   5   6

3) *Hidari mae empi-uchi*

Deliver a left front elbow strike to the right side. Turn only the upper body to perform the technique, striking the elbow against the palm of the right hand. The lower body remains in a proper straddle-leg stance.

4) Turn the head to the left while drawing the right fist down to above the right hip, simultaneously dropping the left fist on top of the right fist so that the back of the left hand faces outward.

5) *Hidari gedan-barai*

Perform a left downward block to the left side.

6) *Migi chūdan kagi-zuki*

Deliver a right middle-level hook punch to the left side. The fist travels along a course parallel to the floor and level with the solar plexus. The right elbow is bent so that the forearm is parallel to the hips upon completion.

7) Without moving the upper body or raising the hips, draw the right foot in front of the left leg, placing it on the far side of the left foot to assume a cross-legged stance.

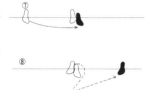

• Swing the left leg up in front of the body toward the right side while driving the right fist back over the left shoulder and turning the head to face the front. During this movement the left foot and the right fist move in opposite directions, twisting the upper body to generate momentum for the following technique.

7   8

8) *Hidari fumikomi/Migi chūdan uchi ude-uke*

Deliver a left stamping kick to the left side, shifting into a straddle-leg stance while performing a right middle-level inside-to-outside block to the front.

- Keeping both elbows bent, draw the left fist out and upward while pulling the right elbow back and downward, crossing the arms in front of the chest with the left arm traveling on the far side of the right arm.

9) *Hidari jōdan nagashi-uke/Migi gedan-barai*

Pull the left elbow back behind the shoulder, drawing the left fist back to beside the left ear with the back of the hand facing inward to perform a left upper-level sweeping block. At the same time, thrust the right arm down in front of the body to execute a right downward block.

| 9 | 10 | 11a | 11b |

10) *Hidari jōdan uraken-uchi*

Pull the right fist back toward the body at the height of the solar plexus while delivering a left upper-level back-fist strike targeting the opponent's face. The right fist supports the left elbow at the moment of impact for a more powerful strike. The *nagashi-uke/gedan-barai* and *uraken-uchi* in movements 9 and 10 are performed in one continuous motion.

11a) *Hidari nami-gaeshi*

Keeping the arms in place, turn the head to the left and then immediately snap the left foot up toward the lower abdomen to perform a left return-wave kick, a swift kicking motion that is initiated in a manner similar to performing a leg sweep (*ashi-barai*). Neither the hips nor center of gravity should move during the return-wave kick.

11b) *Hidari sokumen-uke*

Plant the left foot on the floor and perform a side block to the left with the left arm, keeping the back of the right fist in contact with the bottom of the left elbow. Turn only the upper body to perform the technique while maintaining a proper straddle-leg stance.

12a   12b   13   14

12a) *Migi nami-gaeshi*

Keeping the arms in place, turn the head to the right and then perform a right return-wave kick.

12b) *Hidari sokumen-uke*

Plant the right foot on the floor and then execute a side block to the right with the left arm, turning only the upper body to perform the technique. The lower body maintains a proper straddle-leg stance and the right fist stays positioned below the left elbow.

13) Turn the head to the left while drawing both fists down to above the right hip.

14) *Morote-zuki*

Deliver a double-fist punch to the left side with a *kiai*. The left fist is level with the shoulder and the right fist is level with the solar plexus.

• Open the left hand and draw it back across the chest and below the right under-arm.

15   16   17

15) *Hidari chūdan haishu-uke*

Slowly draw the left hand out to the left side to perform a middle-level back-hand block.

16) *Migi mae empi-uchi*

Deliver a right front elbow strike to the left side, striking the elbow against the palm of the left hand.

17) Turn the head to the right while dropping both fists down to above the left hip.

18   19   20   21

18) *Migi gedan-barai*

Perform a right downward block to the right side.

19) *Hidari chūdan kagi-zuki*

Deliver a left middle-level hook punch to the right side.

20) Without moving the upper body or raising the hips, draw the left foot in front of the right leg, placing it on the far side of the right foot to assume a cross-legged stance.

• Swing the right leg up in front of the body toward the left side while thrusting the left fist back over the right shoulder and turning the head to face the front. (As in the motion prior to movement 8, simultaneously driving the right foot and left hand in opposite directions serves to twist the upper body, which offers remedial exercise for the spine.)

21) *Migi fumikomi/Hidari chūdan uchi ude-uke*

Deliver a right stamping kick to the right side, shifting into a straddle-leg stance while performing a left middle-level inside-to-outside block to the front.

22   23

- Keeping both elbows bent, draw the right fist out and upward while pulling the left elbow back and downward, crossing the arms in front of the chest with the right arm traveling on the far side of the left arm.

22) *Migi jōdan nagashi-uke/Hidari gedan-barai*

Draw the right arm back to the right side of the body to perform a right upper-level sweeping block while thrusting the left arm down toward the front to execute a left downward block.

23) *Migi jōdan uraken-uchi*

Pull the left fist back toward the body while delivering a right upper-level back-fist strike. The left fist provides support underneath the right elbow at the moment of impact. Movements 22 and 23 are performed in one continuous motion.

24a) *Migi nami-gaeshi*

Keeping the arms in place, turn the head to the right and immediately perform a right return-wave kick.

24b) *Migi sokumen-uke*

Plant the right foot on the floor and, turning only the upper body, execute a side block to the right with the right arm, keeping the left fist positioned underneath the right elbow.

24a   24b   25a   25b

25a) **Hidari nami-gaeshi**

Keeping the arms in place, turn the head to the left and then perform a left return-wave kick.

25b) **Migi sokumen-uke**

Plant the left foot on the floor and execute a side block to the left with the right arm, turning only the upper body to perform the technique while keeping the left fist in contact with the right elbow.

26) Turn the head to the right while drawing both fists down to above the left hip.

27) **Morote-zuki**

Deliver a double-fist punch to the right side with a *kiai*.

28) **Yame**

Naore

(*Naore* is a command to return to a natural-posture stance.)

- Draw the right foot inward into a closed parallel stance and bring the hands together in front of the body as in the initial ready position, with the left hand over the right hand.
- Maintain a state of physical and mental readiness (*zanshin*).

26   27   28

GLOSSARY OF JAPANESE KARATE TERMS

General

Ashi: Foot, leg

Bokutō: Wooden sword

Bu-dō: Martial arts

Chūdan: Middle level of the body (chest area)

-dō: Suffix meaning path or way (as in *sa-dō* [Japanese tea ceremony; literally "the way of tea"] and *ka-dō* [Japanese flower arranging; "the way of flowers"])

Dōjo: Training hall

Dōjo-kun: The five precepts constituting karate's code of ethics (literal translation: code of ethics for the training hall)

Embusen: Performance line (a pattern formed by the movements that make up a *kata*)

Empi: Elbow (also *hiji*)

Fukuwan: "Belly" arm (the anterior surface of the forearm leading into the palm)

Gedan: Lower level of the body, downward

Gohon kumite: Five-step *kumite*

Gyaku: Reverse or opposite

Haisoku: Instep

Haitō: Ridge hand

Haiwan: Back arm (the posterior surface of the forearm leading into the back of the hand)

Hara: Lower abdomen, located roughly 8 cm (a little over 3 inches) below the navel (also *seika-tanden, tanden*)

Hidari: Left

Hiji: Elbow (also *empi*)

Hiza: Knee

Ichigeki hissatsu: To kill with a single strike

Ippon-kumite: One-step *kumite*

Jiyū ippon kumite: Free-style one-step *kumite*

Jiyū kumite: Free sparring

Jōdan: Upper level of the body (face area)

Kakato: Heel of the foot

Kamae: Ready position

Karate-dō: Way or path of karate

Kata: Pre-arranged forms comprising a series of offensive and defensive techniques that are performed individually against imaginary opponents

Keri: Kick (pronounced *geri* when preceded by another word, as in *mae-geri*)

Kiai: A loud vocalization, such as "*yaah*," timed to coincide with a decisive technique

Kihon: Basic, the basics

Kihon ippon kumite: Basic one-step *kumite*

Ki-o-tsuke: Call to attention

Kizami: Refers to a technique performed using the arm or leg positioned in front

Kobudō: Traditional fighting arts

Kobushi: Fist

Koshi: Ball of the foot

Kumite: Sparring

Maai: Distance maintained between opponents during *kumite*

Mae: Front, forward

Makiwara: Punching board

Migi: Right

Mokusō: Silent meditation

Naore: Command to return to a natural-posture stance

Seika-tanden: Lower abdomen, located roughly 8 cm (a little over 3 inches) below the navel (also *tanden, hara*)

Seiza: A traditional Japanese style of sitting, with the legs folded underneath, the buttocks resting on the heels, and the tops of the feet against the floor

Shihō-wari: Board breaking in four directions

Sokusō: Tips of toes

Sokutei: Sole of the foot

Sokutō: Foot edge

Sonoba-zuki: Punching while standing in place

Soto: Outside, outside-to-inside

Soto-ude: Outer arm (the little-finger side of the forearm)

Sun-dome: Bringing attacks to a sudden halt one *sun* (about 3 cm, or 1¼ inches) before making contact with the target

Tachi: Stance (pronounced *dachi* when preceded by another word, as in *zenkutsu-dachi*)

Tai-sabaki: Body shifting

Tameshi-wari: Testing the effectiveness of a technique by attempting to break boards, tiles, etc.

Tanden: Lower abdomen, located roughly 8 cm (a little over 3 inches) below the navel (also *seika-tanden, hara*)

Tate: Vertical

Te: Hand

Tenshin: Body rotation

Tsuki: Punch (pronounced *zuki* when preceded by another word, as in *gyaku-zuki*)

Uchi: 1. Strike; 2. Inside, inside-to-outside

Uchi-ude: Inner arm (the thumb side of the forearm)

Ude: Arm

Uke: Block

Unsoku: Leg movement (the use of the legs when advancing, retreating, etc.)

Ushiro: Back, rear

Yakusoku kumite: Promise sparring, in which the attacking technique and target are predetermined

Yōi: Call to assume a ready position

Yoko: Side, horizontal

Zanshin: A state of physical and mental preparedness following the performance of a technique

Stances

Fudō-dachi: Rooted stance
Gyaku-hanmi: Reverse half-front-facing position (hips at a 45-degree angle to the front, with the hip on the side opposite to the front leg pushed forward)
Hachiji-dachi: Open V stance (also *soto hachiji-dachi*)
Hangetsu-dachi: Half-moon stance
Hanmi: Half-front-facing position (hips at a 45-degree angle to the front)
Heikō-dachi: Open parallel stance
Heisoku-dachi: Closed parallel stance
Hidari zenkutsu-dachi: Left front stance
Kamae: Ready position
Kiba-dachi: Straddle-leg stance
Kōkutsu-dachi: Back stance
Kōsa-dachi: Cross-legged stance
Migi zenkutsu-dachi: Right front stance
Musubi-dachi: Closed V stance
Neko ashi-dachi: Cat stance
Renoji-dachi: L stance
Sanchin-dachi: Hourglass stance
Shiko-dachi: Square stance
Shizentai: Natural posture
Soto hachiji-dachi: Open V stance (also *hachiji-dachi*)
Tachi: Stance (pronounced *dachi* when preceded by another word, as in *zenkutsu-dachi*)
Zenkutsu-dachi: Front stance

Hand/Arm Techniques

Age-uke: Rising block
Awase seiryūtō-uke: Two-handed ox-jaw block
Choku-zuki: Straight punch
Chūdan shutō-uke: Middle-level knife-hand block
Chūdan soto ude-uke: Middle-level outside-to-inside block (also *chūdan soto-uke*)
Chūdan soto-uke: Middle-level outside-to-inside block (also *chūdan soto ude-uke*)
Chūdan uchi ude-uke: Middle-level inside-to-outside block (also *chūdan uchi-uke*)
Chūdan uchi-uke: Middle-level inside-to-outside block (also *chūdan uchi ude-uke*)
Empi: Elbow (also *hiji*)
Empi-uchi: Elbow strike (also *hiji-ate*)
Fukuwan: "Belly" arm (the anterior surface of the forearm leading into the palm)
Gedan-barai: Downward block
Gedan seiken jūji-uke: Downward fist X-block
Gyaku uchi-uke: Reverse inside-to-outside block
Gyaku-zuki: Reverse punch
Haishu: Back hand
Haishu jūji-uke: Back-hand X-block
Haishu-uke: Back-hand block
Haitō: Ridge hand

Haiwan: Back arm (the posterior surface of the forearm leading into the back of the hand)
Haiwan-uke: Back-arm block
Hiji: Elbow (also *empi*)
Hiji-ate: Elbow strike (also *empi-uchi*)
Hiraken: Fore-knuckle fist
Ippon-ken: One-knuckle fist
Jōdan age-uke: Upper-level rising block
Jōdan haishu jūji-uke: Upper-level back-hand X-block
Jōdan shutō jūji-uchi: Upper-level knife-hand X-strike
Jūji-uke: X-block
Jun-zuki: Front punch
Kagi-zuki: Hook punch
Kakutō: Bent wrist
Keitō: Chicken-head wrist
Kizami-zuki: Jab
Kobushi: Fist
Kumade: Bear hand
Mae empi-uchi: Front elbow strike
Mae mawashi empi-uchi: Forward round elbow strike
Mawashi empi-uchi: Round elbow strike
Morote-uke: Augmented block
Morote-zuki: Double-fist punch
Nagashi-uke: Sweeping block
Nakadaka ippon-ken: Middle-finger one-knuckle fist
Nihon-nukite: Two-finger spear hand
Nukite: Spear hand
Oi-zuki: Lunge punch
Osae-uke: Pressing block
Otoshi empi-uchi: Downward elbow strike
Sanbon-zuki: Three-punch combination
Seiken: Fore fist, fist
Seiken jūji-uke: Fist X-block
Seiryūtō: Ox-jaw hand
Seiryūtō-uke: Ox-jaw block
Shihon-nukite: Four-finger spear hand
Shutō: Knife hand
Shutō jūji-uchi: Knife-hand X-strike
Shutō-uchi: Knife-hand strike
Shutō-uke: Knife-hand block
Sokumen-uke: Side block
Sonoba-zuki: Punching while standing in place
Soto-mawashi shutō-uchi: Outside round knife-hand strike
Soto-ude: Outer arm (the little-finger side of the forearm)
Soto ude-uke: Outside-to-inside block (also *soto-uke*)
Soto-uke: Outside-to-inside block (also *soto ude-uke*)
Sukui-uke: Scooping block
Tate empi-uchi: Upward elbow strike
Tate-mawashi tettsui-uchi: Vertical round hammer-fist strike
Tate-mawashi uraken-uchi: Vertical round back-fist strike
Tate shutō-uke: Vertical knife-hand block
Tate-zuki: Vertical-fist punch
Te: Hand
Teishō: Palm heel
Tettsui: Hammer fist

Tettsui-uchi: Hammer-fist strike

Tsuki: Punch (pronounced *zuki* when preceded by another word, as in *gyaku-zuki*)

Uchi: Strike

Uchi haiwan-uke: Inside-to-outside back-arm block

Uchi-mawashi shutō-uchi: Inside round knife-hand strike

Uchi-ude: Inner arm (the thumb side of the forearm)

Uchi ude-uke: Inside-to-outside block (also *uchi-uke*)

Uchi-uke: Inside-to-outside block (also *uchi ude-uke*)

Ude: Arm

Uke: Block

Uraken: Back fist

Uraken-uchi: Back-fist strike

Ura-zuki: Close punch

Ushiro empi-uchi: Back elbow strike

Ushiro-mawashi empi-uchi: Back round elbow strike

Washide: Eagle hand

Yoko empi-uchi: Side elbow strike

Yokoken: Side fist

Yoko-mawashi tettsui-uchi: Side round hammer-fist strike

Yoko-mawashi uraken-uchi: Side round back-fist strike

Leg/Foot Techniques

Ashi: Foot, leg

Ashi-barai: Leg sweep

Fumikomi: Stamping kick

Gyaku mikazuki-geri: Reverse crescent kick

Haisoku: Top of the foot, from the ankle to above the toes

Hiza: Knee

Jōhaisoku: Area around the top of the toes

Kakato: Heel

Kekomi: Thrust kick

Keri: Kick (pronounced *geri* when preceded by another word, as in *mae-geri*)

Kesa-geri: Jumping side kick (also *tobi yoko-geri*)

Kizami-geri: Short kick (kick using the front leg)

Kizami mawashi-geri: Short roundhouse kick (using the front leg)

Koshi: Ball of the foot

Mae-geri: Front snap kick

Mawashi-geri: Roundhouse kick

Mikazuki-geri: Crescent kick

Nami-gaeshi: Return-wave kick

Nidan-geri: Double jump kick

Ren-geri: Consecutive kicks

Sokusō: Tips of toes

Sokutei: Sole

Sokutō: Foot edge

Tobi-geri: Jumping kick

Tobi mae-geri: Jumping front kick

Tobi mawashi-geri: Jumping roundhouse kick

Tobi yoko-geri: Jumping side kick (also *kesa-geri*)

Unsoku: Leg movement (the use of the legs when advancing, retreating, etc.)

Ushiro-geri: Back kick

Ushiro mawashi-geri: Back roundhouse kick

Yoko-geri: Side kick

Yoko-geri ke-age: Side snap kick (also *yoko ke-age*)

Yoko-geri kekomi: Side thrust kick (also *yoko-kekomi*)

Yoko ke-age: Side snap kick (also *yoko-geri ke-age*)

Yoko-kekomi: Side thrust kick (also *yoko-geri kekomi*)

Yori-ashi: A sliding motion of the feet as a result of thrusting off one foot to propel the body in a given direction

Nunchaku techniques

Chūdan yama-gamae: Middle-level mountain position

Dai-jōdan gamae: Upper open position

Fūsha-gaeshi: Windmill strike

Gedan jūji-uke: Lower-level X-block

Gyaku shajō-gaeshi: Reverse diagonal strike

Gyaku shihō-uke: Reverse square block

Hapū-gaeshi: Figure-eight strike

Ichimonji gamae: Upper-level horizontal position (also *jōdan suihei gamae*)

Jōdan age-uke: Upper-level rising block

Jōdan gyaku age-uke: Upper-level reverse rising block

Jōdan suihei gamae: Upper-level horizontal position (also *ichimonji gamae*)

Jōdan yama-gamae: Upper-level mountain position

Jūji-uke: X-block

Komata-gaeshi: Inner-thigh reversal

Musubi-gamae: Entangled position

Omote sempūrin: Front whirlwind

Seigan no kamae: Engagement position

Shajō-gaeshi: Diagonal strike

Sokumen jōdan gamae: Upper flank position

Tsubame-gaeshi: Swallow strike

Ura sempūrin: Rear whirlwind

Yama-gamae: Mountain position